POKéMON™

Prima's Official Strategy Guide

Project Editor: Brooke N. Raymond

ISBN: 7615-2282-4
Library of Congress Catalog Card Number: 98-067343
Printed in the United States of America

99 00 01 02 GG 10 9 8 7 6 5 4 3 2

Elizabeth M. Hollinger
Maps created by: James M. Ratkos

PRIMA PUBLISHING
Rocklin, California
(916) 632-4400

Acknowledgments

This book has been a real labor of love. There is no way that I could have ever completed this mammoth project with out the help and support of many people. Thanks are owed to:

—The staff at Prima, especially Jon, Stacy, and most of all Brooke, for dealing with me in those moments of pique, frustration, and stress. You do a good job and I'm grateful, even when grumpy.

—Nintendo of America, for deciding to bring this wonderful game to the states. Thanks to Juana Tingdale and Cammy Budd for all their support on our Nintendo products. Thanks are also due to Ellen Enrico, Michael Kelbaugh, and Bill Giese for all of their hard work and reams of information. And especially to Bill for the awesome Mewtwo toy!

—Ryan Li, my Pokémon e-mail pal, for all of the strategic discussions about the later stages of the game. Congratulations on getting all 150 pocket monsters!

—My mom, for giving up the first part of her vacation with me. I really appreciate your patience and support.

—And, most importantly, my partner in crime, Jim Ratkos for the meticulously crafted maps for which he gave up much sleep and other free time. You're a great friend and I appreciate your contribution more than you'll ever understand.

Contents

How I Became a Pokémaniac ii

How to Become a Master Pokémon Trainer 1

A Walk Through the World of Pokémon 7

The Complete Pokédex 62

All the Skills You Ever Need to Know 79

Items Galore! 84

A Pokémon Check-List 89

How I Became a Pokémaniac

As a writer of strategy guides, I find myself playing a lot of games—but rarely for fun and entertainment (as is often the case when a pastime becomes a job). But in March 1998, my writing partner and I found a place where we could order copies of a Japanese game called Pocket Monsters. With rumors floating around about a possible American release, we picked up this mysterious little game not knowing what we were in for. In fact, it sat unopened on my bookshelf for almost a month until I found myself on a plane from Michigan to California with nothing to do. By the return flight, I was hooked and found myself playing this game everywhere and anywhere, from my bedroom in the wee hours of the morning to the checkout line at my local grocery store. There was something about Pokémon (as it's now called), that sucked me in and kept me playing even when I was supposed to be doing other things.

So what is Pokémon, and why is it so addictive that more than eight million copies of this game have been sold in Japan? Ultimately, Pokémon is a role-playing game, but it's also much more. It's a game that is both simple and complex at the same time. It's a game about collecting monsters (150 of them, to be precise), which encourages you to look to others for help in getting the missing pieces. Pokémon is also about raising monsters and about strategy and fighting for a cause.

Its appeal lies in the fact that there's always something new to do or accomplish. It's never boring, and there are always new challenges waiting on the horizon. You can fight against established Trainers for Badges that will boost your abilities in some way or explore caves for treasure or rare, legendary Pokémon. Even those "Random Battles" prove helpful when you're scouring the countryside for new Wild Pokémon or trying to get a favorite monster to its next evolution point. And the portable size of the Game Boy® means you can take it with you anywhere!

So, sit back, relax, and enjoy your stay in the world of Pokémon. And don't be concerned if it takes over your life. It's supposed to!

How to Become a Master Pokémon Trainer

Welcome to the world of Pokémon! Once you start this game, you'll find yourself immersed in a world that is as challenging as it is fun. Your mission: To become the world's greatest Pokémon Trainer. To do this, you'll have to wander down many streets and through cities, towns, and dungeons—and defeat many Rivals, including the one who used to be your best friend. You also have to find and collect 150 Pokémon and raise some of them to be your bettermost fighters. It takes skill and determination, not to mention a bit of luck. But if you follow the advice given in these pages, you should have no problem!

Note

It's highly recommended that you read the game manual to familiarize yourself with the basics of gameplay. The purpose of this chapter is not to repeat the instructions, but rather to expand on them and give you more advanced techniques.

The Red vs. Blue Question

So, what's the difference between the Red and Blue versions of the game? In a nutshell, the two games are very similar. They have the same characters, the same plot, and the same map. The differences are in the assortment of Pokémon that each version of the cartridge contains.

I. Each version of the game contains 11 unique Pokémon.

Red Version	Blue Version
Ekans	Sandshrew
Arbok	Sandslash
Oddish	Meowth
Gloom	Persian
Vileplume	Bellsprout
Mankey	Weepinbell
Primeape	Victreebel
Growlithe	Vulpix
Arcanine	Ninetales
Scyther	Magmar
Electabuzz	Pinsir

II. The Pokémon you can buy at the Coin Exchange (and their prices) differ in each version.

Red Version		Blue Version	
Abra	180CR	Abra	120CR
Clefairy	500CR	Clefairy	750CR
Nidorina	1,200CR	Nidorino	1,200CR
Dratini	2,800CR	Pinsir	2,500CR
Scyther	5,500CR	Dratini	4,600CR
Porygon	9,999CR	Porygon	6,500CR

You'll also find that some species of Pokémon appear in one place in the Red version, but somewhere else in the Blue version. For example, you'll find Horsea and Seadra in the Seafoam Islands in the Red version of the game, but Krabby and Kingler in the Blue version.

Also, certain Pokémon appear more frequently in one version than the other. There are more Weedle and Kakuna in the Red version and Caterpie and Metapod in the Blue. More female Nidoran roam the thickets of the Blue version of Pokémon than male, while you'll be beating male Nidoran off with a stick in the Red version of the game. Get the picture?

Should these differences affect the color of the game you buy? Well, that's a matter of personal taste. If there's a certain unique monster that you must have, then pick up the version that contains that monster. If you like the color red more than blue, grab the red one. The monster sets in both version of the game are equal in terms of strength and elemental mix. And if you're planning on finding all 150 Pokémon, you'll get to see every single one of them eventually anyway.

Getting Started

When you first boot up Pokémon, you'll be faced with three immediate choices: what to name your character, what to name your Rival, and which Pokémon to start the game with. Of the three, it is the later question which is the most important. Once you've found Prof. Oak, he'll take you back to his Lab, where you can choose one Pokémon from his remaining group of three. Your Rival gets to choose next and then the remaining Poké Ball goes to Prof. Oak (although he'll leave it where it is for the entire game).

But which to choose …? Conventional wisdom says that the Bulbasaur is your best bet. It levels up more quickly than the other two and, being a Grass type, it's extremely effective against the Ground and Water types of Pokémon in the first two Gyms. The Charmander, with its fire and ability to equip strong offensive skills and two of the five Hidden Skills, is my personal choice but it takes the longest to raise and is not very strong against the first two Trainers. However, if you team it up with an Electric Pokémon, like a Pikachu, then you'll have a powerful team that can take on most anything in the game. The same goes for the Squirtle. This character is strong against the Ground Pokémon in the first Gym and can also equip the powerful water-based skill machine given to you when you defeat Misty at the Cerulean City Gym.

Ultimately, you should choose the one that best suits your personality. There really is no correct choice here, so don't worry about making a mistake. Besides, you'll have the opportunity to capture up to 10 more types of Pokémon between Pallet Town and your appointment with Brock at the Pewter City Gym, and you'll want to fill out your team with some of them.

Note

The Pokémon you choose has a direct bearing on which one your Rival ends up with. If you choose the Charmander, your Rival will most likely end up taking the Squirtle. Choose the Bulbasaur and he'll take the Charmander. If you want the Squirtle, he'll settle for the Bulbasaur.

The Art of Capturing Pokémon

You have to know how to capture Pokémon if you want to succeed in this game. There's just no way around it! First, you have to have a Poké Ball, which you can buy at any of the Poké Marts in a town or city near you. Then you have to get into a battle with a Wild Pokémon. The rules of the game state that you can't steal Pokémon from other Trainers, so don't try it or you'll end up wasting a Poké Ball. The only fair game is what you find in the patches of long grass on the routes between towns or in dungeons, forests, ponds (once you have a fishing pole), or caves. You'll also have opportunities to trade people for rare Pokémon, but we'll deal with that later on.

Once you've flushed out a Wild Pokémon, you must weaken it before you can capture it in a Poké Ball. Ideally, you'll want to bring it as close to the point of fainting without actually defeating it before using your Poké Ball. This means that you have to be careful. If you find yourself battling a Pokémon that you really want to capture (especially if they don't appear very commonly, like a Pikachu or Clefairy), don't send your strongest fighters against it or use skills that are sure to defeat it in one round. Choose tamed Pokémon of a similar experience level who you are confident will survive the battle and who can inflict a controllable amount of damage. Skills that produce paralysis or sleep are also good ways to ensure that you don't miss.

As you progress through the game, you'll be able to buy more effective versions of the basic Poké Ball that will work better against the more powerful monsters. Don't expect to have an easier time capturing Pokémon, though. The contents of Poké Marts change to correspond with the level of Pokémon and challenges that you will meet up with in that section of the game. Using an Ultra Ball, which is the most effective Poké Ball that you can buy in a store, on a LV2 Spearow will certainly guarantee your chances of capturing that creature (unless you let your LV30+ Pokémon attack it), but don't even consider using a basic Poké Ball against one of the legendary bird trio or that LV70 Mewtwo! In fact, extremely rare and powerful Pokémon like the bird trio of Articuno, Zapdos, and Moltres; the awesome Mewtwo; or even the sleepy Snorlax will often require you to toss somewhere in the neighborhood of 50 Ultra Balls before you can capture them! This game is less about strength than it is about patience and cunning.

The Care and Feeding of Your Pokémon

For the most part, taking care of a troop of Pokémon is pretty easy as long as you remember to heal its wounds and take it for regular checkups at the many Pokémon Centers throughout the land. Still, there are a few extra things involved in raising a Pokémon that is more than just "fighting fit."

There is a reason why people say that a trained Pokémon is stronger than a Wild Pokémon of the same experience level. When you train a Pokémon of your own you have a great amount of influence over its development. You decide whether or not it evolves at certain points, which skills it learns, etc. Captured Pokémon also receive bonuses to their attack and defense strengths, speed, and special skills from the Badges you've collected. You can customize your Pokémon further by equipping them with skills from Technical Machines (TMs) or Hidden Machines (HMs) and by feeding them attribute-raising vitamins and minerals like Calcium, Iron, Carbos, etc.

It's also better, whenever possible, to raise Pokémon from a young age. A Chansey caught in the Safari Zone at the relatively low level of 23 and raised to LV 50+ will have better overall stats and be much stronger than an LV50+ one caught in the Unknown Dungeon. When presented with the choice of keeping a self-taught monster or replacing it with a newly caught version with a slightly higher experience level, be sure to check out its stats and collection of skills—I think you'll be surprised by what you find.

When you raise a Pokémon from a lower level, you also have more control over when it evolves. Pushing the B Button during an evolution sequence will prevent the Pokémon from changing into the next form. There are pros and cons to doing this however. A first-form Pokémon has the ability to learn skills much faster than its more evolved cousins. For example, a Squirtle can learn the powerful Hydro Pump skill at LV 42, while the Wartortle will have to wait until he reaches LV 47 and the Blastoise until LV 52—10 levels later! If you're raising a Pokémon that evolves by means other than leveling up (i.e., with an Element Stone or by trading), there is a chance that evolution will keep them from learning any new skills at all or will make them learn a whole new set. On the other hand, evolution tends to make Pokémon stronger and more flexible. Many times, reaching a new stage will allow a Pokémon to use different TMs or learn more powerful skills. There are a few Pokémon, like the Magikarp, that evolution will change from a weaker creature to a frightening and all-powerful monster. Make sure that you know your Pokémon before deciding how to raise them!

Note

You don't have to raise all of your low-level Pokémon if you don't want to. But if you decide that you really want a certain Pokémon in your main group of monsters, it's better to grab one while it's young than to wait until you can capture it at a higher level. Also, there are some Pokémon that appear in the later stages of the game where you won't have that luxury; there are also some Pokémon that you won't want to use regardless of what level you can capture them at.

Evolution

Most Pokémon change forms as they grow more experienced. Some Pokémon will even evolve twice before they reach their final form, while others won't evolve at all. There are three types of evolution in the world of Pokémon—leveling up, use of an Elemental Stone, and trading them to another cartridge—and since a Pokémon's method of evolution does have an effect on how often they appear in the game, it's a good idea to understand the fundamentals of Pokémon evolution.

Leveling Up

There are 36 species of Pokémon that reach their second or third form through the simple act of gaining experience and leveling up. This is the most fundamental way that Pokémon evolve and also the most time consuming. It should come as no surprise then to find out that you'll find the majority of these 36 species and even many of their evolved cousins roaming about in the wild. If you're trying to collect all 150 Pokémon, raise only those that you want to play an active role in your party and try to capture as many forms of the others as you can.

Elemental Stones

Many Pokémon can be coaxed into evolving with the use of an Elemental Stone. Four of the five stones (Fire, Water, Leaf, Thunder, and Moon) can be found in Item Balls in dungeons or bought at the Celadon Dept. Store. The Moon Stone is the rarest of them all and is found in dungeons only. Because your quantity of these is limited, use them wisely. You won't be able to evolve all of the Pokémon who need them! Seventeen species in all grow with the use of Elemental Stones.

Note

Evolving a Pokémon with an Elemental Stone is risky business. The majority of creatures who evolve this way will either lose their ability to pick up learned skills or will learn different skills than those set for the first or second form. Because you can use the stones at any time, its a good idea to wait until the Pokémon is well trained and then upgrade the monster.

Note

Unlike Pokémon who evolve through the use of Elemental Stones, the four Pokémon brought about by trading aren't penalized when it comes to learning new skills. In fact, they retain the same learning rate as their second-form counterparts.

Trading

There are four species of Pokémon that evolve suddenly and mysteriously when you trade them with a friend at the Link Cable Club. All four species (Abra, Machop, Geodude, and Gastly) have three different forms, the second of which is reached by leveling the Pokémon up. Once they've reached that second form, you can trade them at any time. Once the Poké Ball has traveled through the Link Cable, the transformation will begin!

Pokémon That Don't Evolve

There are 24 Pokémon that don't face evolution, and they are all rare and precious creatures. Most of them only appear once in dungeons or in in-game trade scenarios, while a few can be found only in special areas like the Safari Zone.

The Importance of Trading

If you want to become a Master Pokémon Trainer, you have to be willing to trade your Pokémon. This is the only way that you'll be able to collect all 150 Pokémon. Within the game itself you'll find four people who are willing to trade their rare Pokémon for your more common ones. When you run across these people, make a note of their location and come back with the Pokémon they've requested. Because they're only looking for common Pokémon, get two and trade them the extra one.

Getting the unique Pokémon from the other version of the game, as well as the Pokémon that you didn't choose in certain parts of the game, requires you to link up with a friend at the Link Cable Club. Remember each version of the game has 11 Pokémon that you will only find on that particular cartridge. So if you want a Meowth and you're playing the Red version of the game, you'll need to find someone with both a Link Cable, a Blue version of the game, and an extra Meowth. You perform trades by going to the Link Cable Club counter at any local Pokémon Center. Enter the Trading Room and sit down at the table to negotiate possible trades. Once you trade a Pokémon, it's gone from your cart until you trade it back. You still retain credit for capturing it in your Pokédex, which opens up the floor for possible "temporary" trades. This works especially well if your friend needs credit for a certain Pokémon that you're unwilling to part with.

Trading Pokémon also has the added benefit of increasing the amount of experience that the traded Pokémon earns in battle. A Pokémon traded to you from another cartridge earns 1.5 times more experience than a normal Pokémon. There are also four types of Pokémon that evolve into their final form only when they're traded across a Link Cable.

A Few Do's and Don'ts Before Playing

Play this Game with a Friend—or Better Yet, Two!
Trading is an integral part of Pokémon, so the sooner you get used to it, the better off you'll be. If you don't want to deal with friends and you have an extra Game Boy and a Link Cable, then buy both versions of the game and trade with yourself.

Regardless of which you choose, getting all 150 Pokémon requires a carefully orchestrated and planned effort and is best done between three people. Here's a list of the points at which you'll need to make plans ahead of time and decide who gets what:

1. The official choosing of starter Pokémon at the beginning of the game.
2. Dome Fossil or Helix Fossil at the bottom of Mt. Moon?
3. Porygon for 9,999CR (Red Version) or 6,500CR (Blue Version)?
4. Hitmonlee or Hitmonchan at the splinter Gym in Saffron City?
5. Evolve Eevee with a Thunder Stone, Water Stone, or Fire Stone?

If you assign each partner a role, then you'll have a much easier time collecting Pokémon without duplicating rare ones.

Don't Concentrate on Raising One Character Over the Others
We all know how it goes. You get a Pokémon that you really like and you use it more often than any of the others. That's fine, but it's better if you share the wealth and experience points for several reasons. A well-balanced team made up of equally strong Pokémon will fare much better against the Elite Four and your Rival. It also guarantees you backup in case your favorite Pokémon runs out of PP or is incapacitated in battle. Remember, as the game progresses the number of Trainers you'll have to defeat in any one area increases too, as does the challenge they present.

Take Advantage of the 1.5 Experience Bonus of Traded Pokémon
If you find yourself with a Pokémon that you need raised in a short amount of time, try trading it to another cartridge. Traded Pokémon receive 1.5 times the experience points of regular Pokémon and they can add up in hurry. This is an especially effective way to level up more powerful Pokémon who evolve at higher levels than normal, like the Dratini.

Don't Try to Play the Game from the Beginning with Your Friend's LV70 Mewtwo

It sounds like a good idea, doesn't it? But, unfortunately, Pokémon has incorporated a system of checks and balances with the Badge system that will encourage you not to do this. As you'll find out from a citizen of Pewter City, Pokémon can choose not to obey a new and inexperienced Trainer. In fact, it is not until you reach Cerulean City and win the Cascade Badge that you are guaranteed mastery over all Pokémon up to LV 30. The Rainbow Badge extends that mastery to LV 50 Pokémon, and the Marsh Badge to LV 70 Pokémon. When you defeat the final Leader and acquire the Earth Badge then all Pokémon, regardless of level, will obey you without hesitation. Until then, traded Pokémon, in addition to captured Pokémon, are very susceptible to this little rule and you'll soon find that the LV 70 Mewtwo that you thought would help you win the game in no time, actually spends most of its time sulking and refusing to perform.

Save Often

Saving has its advantages. If you're defeated by a Trainer or one of the Gym Leaders, you'll be resurrected at the last Pokémon Center visited. But, it'll come at a price—namely, half your money!

We also recommend that you save the game before important battles or when you run across one of the legendary Pokémon like Zapdos or the Mewtwo. Because you only get one chance to capture them, saving allows you to restart if something unforeseen happens, like you run out of Ultra Balls or accidentally defeat them.

Don't Be Fooled; Trading Your Pokémon Doesn't Have to Be Permanent

When you trade a Pokémon, you automatically get credit for having captured it. You won't lose this credit if you trade the Pokémon back to the original owner. So, for those of you who are squeamish at the thought of losing one of your precious monsters, remember to stipulate this as a term of agreement before you trade with your friends.

Remember to Buy Antidotes and Other Curatives Before Entering Dungeons

The worst thing in the world is to lose a fight to a monster who fights by putting your Pokémon to sleep because you didn't have a bottle of Awakening potion. Always stock up on potions, antidotes, and other curatives before venturing into unknown locales!

Don't Forget that Pokémon Can Be Afflicted by Only One Negative Status at a Time

However, if your Pokémon do end up paralyzed or poisoned, think twice before healing them during battle. A paralyzed Pokémon is a hindrance at times, but that status anomaly prevents the enemy from hitting it with something worse, like sleep or ice.

Do Try to Match Pokémon In Battle to Maximize Their Effectiveness

The manual for Pokémon provides you with a chart illustrating all the relationships between the different types of Pokémon. Whenever possible, you'll want to sic Pokémon that have a special affinity against the enemy that appears. If you match your Pokémon well, you'll find that Pokémon that are weaker than the enemy have a fighting chance at beating them because of the attack bonus they receive.

More importantly, the chart will keep you from wasting your Pokémon's time fighting against enemies that it'll have no effect on.

Don't Be Afraid to Change Pokémon In the Midst of Battle

Yes, the old bait and switch is perfectly legal here in the world of Pokémon. If you pick up a Pokémon that is much weaker than your current favorites, don't be afraid to level it up by letting it spend a quick round in battle. In fact, moving it to the top of your list and then swapping it with a more powerful fighter is one of the quickest and safest ways to raise a Pokémon. After all, experience points are equally divided between all of the battle's participants!

Experiment

You won't know what's possible until you try it out for yourself. So don't be afraid to mix and match TMs or raise interesting sounding characters. There's no right or wrong way to become a Master Pokémon Trainer, so just enjoy the game.

A Walk Through the World of Pokémon

Part One: The Quick and Dirty Path

If you just want a quick overview of where to go and who to see, then look no further! What appears on the following two pages is a breakdown of the major events in the order they happen. It'll tell you how to travel through the world as well as what to get and who to see in each area. If you use this guide in conjunction with the map pages that follow, you'll be sure to win the acclaimed title of Master Pokémon Trainer in style.

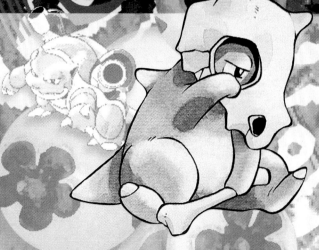

Note

Once you've gotten the Town Map from your Rival's sister, you can use it to get clues as to where to go next. Pushing up on the D-Pad will move the cursor to the next town or route that you should take and, for the most part, will describe the path you must journey before you meet the Elite Four from the Pokémon League.

Pallet Town

◎ Choose one of the three Pokémon in Prof. Oak's Lab.

Route 1: Pallet Town to Viridian City

Viridian City

◎ Pick up Oak's Parcel from the clerk at the Poké Mart.

Route 1: Viridian City to Pallet Town

Pallet Town

◎ Deliver Oak's Parcel to Prof. Oak and receive a Pokédex in exchange.

◎ Pick up a Town Map from your Rival's sister.

Route 1: Pallet Town to Viridian City

Viridian City

Route 2: Viridian City to Pewter City

Viridian Forest

Pewter City

◎ Defeat Brock at the Pewter City Gym.

◎ Get the Boulder Badge.

Route 3: Pewter City to Mt. Moon

Mt. Moon

Route 4: Mt. Moon to Cerulean City

Cerulean City

◎ Defeat Misty at the Cerulean City Gym.

◎ Get the Cascade Badge.

Routes 24 and 25: Cerulean City to Bill's House

Bill's House

◎ Help Bill and get the S.S. Ticket.

Routes 24 and 25: Bill's House to Cerulean City

Cerulean City

Route 5: Cerulean City to Saffron City

Underground Path: Cerulean City to Vermilion City

Route 6: to Vermilion City

Vermilion City

◎ Pick up HM 01 from the Captain of the S.S. Anne.

◎ Defeat Lt. Surge at the Vermilion City Gym.

◎ Get the Thunder Badge.

◎ Pick up the Bike Voucher from the Pokémon Fan Club.

Route 11

Diglett's Cave

Route 2: The Other Side of the Trees

◎ Pick up HM 05.

Diglett's Cave to Route 11 to Vermilion City to Route 6 to the Underground Path and Route 5

Cerulean City

◎ Get the Bicycle with the Bike Voucher.

Route 9: Cerulean City to Rock Tunnel

Rock Tunnel

Route 10: Rock Tunnel to Lavender Town

Lavender Town

Underground Path: Lavender Town to Celadon City

Celadon City
◉ Defeat Erika at the Celadon City Gym.
◉ Get the Rainbow Badge.
◉ Get the Silph Scope from the Team Rocket Hideout beneath the Game Corner.
◉ Buy a Soda Pop from the vending machines on the rooftop of the Celadon Dept. Store.

Underground Path: Cerulean City to Lavender Town

Lavender Town
◉ Rescue Mr. Fuji from the Pokémon Tower.
◉ Get the Poké Flute.

Route 8: Lavender Town to Saffron City
◉ Give the thirsty guard a drink.

Saffron City
◉ Rescue the President of Silph Co. and receive a Master Ball.
◉ Defeat Sabrina at the Saffron City Gym.
◉ Get the Marsh Badge.

Route 7: Saffron City to Celadon City

Celadon City

Route 16
◉ Wake the Snorlax!
◉ Get HM 02 from the house behind the bushes.

Routes 17 and 18: Cycling Road

Route 8: Saffron City to Lavender Town

Lavender Town

Route 12
◉ Wake the Snorlax.

Routes 13, 14, and 15: The Docks

Fuchsia City
◉ Defeat Koga at the Fuchsia City Gym.
◉ Get the Soul Badge.
◉ Pick up HM 03 and the Gold Teeth in the Safari Zone.
◉ Exchange the Gold Teeth for HM 04 with the Game Warden.

Route 19: Fuchsia City to the Seafoam Islands

Seafoam Islands

Route 20: Seafoam Islands to Cinnabar Island

Cinnabar Island
◉ Find the Secret Key in the Pokémon House.
◉ Defeat Blaine at the Cinnabar Island Gym.
◉ Get the Volcano Badge.

Route 21: Cinnabar Island to Pallet Town

Pallet Town and Route 1 to Viridian City

Viridian City
◉ Defeat Giovanni, leader of Team Rocket, at the Viridian City Gym.
◉ Get the Earth Badge.

Route 22 and 23: Viridian City to Victory Road

Victory Road

Indigo Plateau
◉ Defeat the Elite Four, one right after another.
◉ Defeat your Rival one last time.
◉ Become the Master Pokémon Trainer.

The End ... or Is It?

Part Two: A Detailed Look at the World of Pokémon

Pallet Town

This tiny little town is where you were born and raised. Now you're leaving it to go and fulfill your destiny as a Master Pokémon Trainer. Everyone feels a bit sad, but realizes that you must leave the nest sometime. Your goal here is to find the elusive Prof. Oak and earn your first Pokémon.

2. Prof. Oak?

Wanna jump start the game? Then just try leaving Pallet Town. That will make Prof. Oak come running in an instant!

3. The Lab

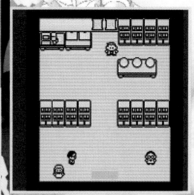

Here in Prof. Oak's lab, you'll receive two things at two different times. First, you'll get your choice from the three Pokémon that the Professor has left in his collection. Hmmm …. Will you take the flowery Bulbasaur, the water-squirting Squirtle, or the fiery Charmander? Whichever you choose, be prepared to defend yourself against your Rival from next door. That bully just won't leave you alone. Later on, once you've delivered a certain Parcel to Prof. Oak, you'll get your Pokédex and be able to buy Poké Balls and start your collection of Pokémon! Happy hunting.

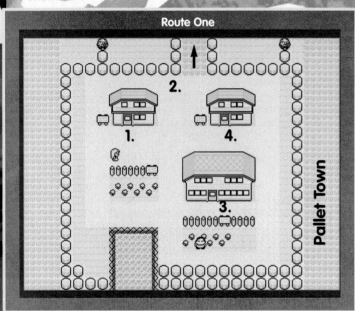

Route One

Pallet Town

4. Why Should You Visit Your Rival's Home?

I don't know, maybe his sister has a crush on you or something. Pay her a visit after you get your Pokédex and she'll give you a copy of the Town Map. This item is awesome and will help you get from town to town!

1. A Little Bit of Home-Cooked Goodness

Inside your house, you'll find the usual luxuries that will remind you of being "home." Upstairs is your SNES and computer, where you'll find a Potion tucked away for just this occasion. Downstairs in the living room, you'll find your mother, who's always willing to provide comfort and a healing dose of chicken soup when you need it. If you're in the neighborhood, pay her a visit and she'll heal your wounds for free!

Pallet Town

Things to Do
◎ Choose a Pokémon.
◎ Deliver Prof. Oak's Parcel and get a Pokédex.
◎ Pick up the Town Map.

Places to Go
◎ Home
◎ Your Rival's Home
◎ Prof. Oak's Lab

Things to Get
◎ Potion
◎ Town Map
◎ Pokédex

Any Pokémon?
◎ Bulbasaur
◎ Charmander
◎ Squirtle
◎ And fish for Poliwag and Goldeen once you get a Fishing Rod.

The roads here in the world of Pokémon can be pretty dangerous if you aren't prepared. The first time you'll walk down this road, it'll just be you and your first Pokémon. But after you gain the ability to capture wild Pokémon, you can use this as a breeding ground. Take this road north to Viridian City.

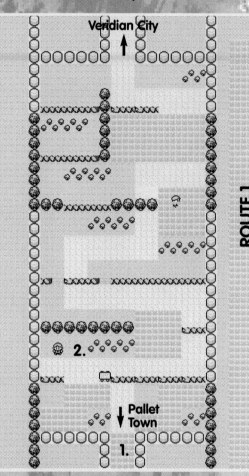

Route 1

1. The Dangers of Long Grass
Wherever you see these thatches of long wavy grass, you'll find Wild Pokémon. It never fails and, with the exception of dungeons and the water, you won't find Wild Pokémon anywhere else! So … if your Pokémon is low on Hit Points or you don't want to fight in any more random battles, stay out of the grass.

2. The Rewards of Being Friendly
Whenever you encounter a person in a town or on a road, take the time to talk with them. They usually have helpful words of wisdom to share or even, in the case of this guy, a spare item.

Tip

This is the first opportunity you'll have to fight Wild Pokémon. The first time up and down this road, you won't have the use of Poké Balls to capture Pokémon or be able to buy a whole lot of Potions to heal you so you'll need to fight with care. If your Pokémon is getting low on health, use your Potion or stay out of the long grass and avoid battles until you can heal them at a Pokémon Center or your own house.

Route 1

Things To Get
👁 Potion

Any Pokémon?

	Red	Blue
Pidgey	Common	Common
Rattata	Common	Common

Viridian City

At first, you won't find much to do here since the Gym's closed up tight. But you will get to visit your first Pokémon Center and shop at a Poké Mart. It's a shame they're out of Potions, though.

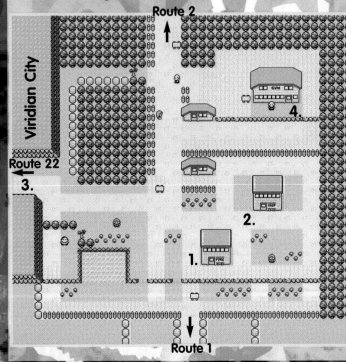

1. My Pokémon Needs Help!

Whenever you enter a new city, one of the first places you'll want to locate is the Pokémon Center. Here you can heal your Pokémon for free at the first counter. Just leave your wounded fighters with the attendant, and she'll return them to you in "fighting fit" form. You can also use the computer terminal here to log into your personal Computer (to store items), Someone's Computer (to store Pokémon), and Prof. Oak's Computer (to have your Pokédex evaluated). A good Pokémon Trainer uses these tools wisely and often—especially since you can only carry twenty items and six Pokémon with you.

The counter to the right is where you'll find the Link Cable Club. Come here whenever you want to trade Pokémon with friends or just battle them head to head in the Coliseum!

Note

Whenever you go out capturing Pokémon, your six slots are filled up first. Then, any extra Pokémon are teleported into storage on your Computer account. Pokémon can be saved this way until the box you've currently selected becomes full. When you know you're going to be entering an area with a lot of new Pokémon, like the Safari Zone, it's a good idea to stop by a Pokémon Center and exchange for an empty box.

2. Delivery for Prof. Oak

Here at the Viridian City Poké Mart, you'll find not only shelves of basic supplies, but a post office as well. The clerk has a package for Prof. Oak that must be delivered immediately and his delivery boy's out sick! Maybe if you do this favor for him now, he'll let you come back and buy some supplies for your long journey ahead.

Merchandise

Poké Ball	200P
Antidote	100P
Paralyze Heal	200P
Burn Heal	250P
Potion	Sold out!

3. Pokémon Hunting on Route 22

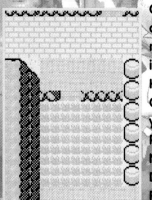

Once you can buy Poké Balls and capture Wild Pokémon, you might want to consider hunting in the long grasses of Route 22. Here, not too far from Viridian City and the Pokémon Center, you'll find lots of low-level Pidgey, Rattata, Spearow, Nidoran ♂, and Nidoran ♀. Don't go too far though. Your Rival is lurking along the path to the top and is dying to challenge you to another fight. Before accepting his challenge, make sure that you have at least two Pokémon trained to LV 9 or above. Your Rival will have two on his side: a LV 9 Pidgey and his default Pokémon at LV 8.

Note

Before you go up against any type of Trainer or Gym Leader, you'll want to make sure that you've spent some time fighting random battles and capturing Wild Pokémon. A good rule of thumb is to make sure that you have as many Pokémon ready to fight as the Trainer does and that they are all at least at the same level of experience if not higher! This may be overkill, but it will prevent you from fainting most of the time.

4. The Gym Is Closed?

Yup, and it will stay that way until you've defeated the other seven Gym Leaders. Sorry. Come back later.

Gym Leader Lowdown #8: Giovanni of the Viridian City Gym

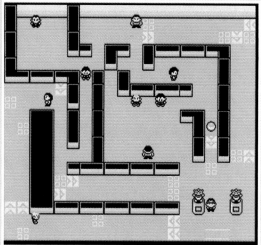

We're jumping the gun a bit here! You won't battle this Trainer officially until the end of the game, so if you don't want to know about him mark this page and come back to it later.

Giovanni is the leader of Team Rocket, and boy is he mad at you! All the Junior Trainers in his Gym are dedicated to Ground Pokémon of the highest levels. When you do pay this Gym a visit on your way to the final confrontation at Indigo Plateau, make sure that you have your best Water, Grass, or Ice Pokémon ready to go and at least at LV 50. Giovanni's Pokémon are mean, and the twisty corridors and transport pads at this Gym will ensure that his Trainers wear you down first.

If you win, you'll get the Earth Badge, which will compel Pokémon of any level to obey your commands and TM 27, the awesome skill Fissure.

Giovanni's Pokémon Lineup

Rhyhorn	LV45
Dugtrio	LV42
Nidoqueen	LV44
Nidoking	LV45
Rhydon	LV50

POKéMON™

Viridian City

Things to Do
- Pick up Oak's Parcel at the Poké Mart.
- Defeat Giovanni at the Gym (much later in the game).

Places to Go
- Pokémon Center
- Poké Mart
- Viridian City Gym

Things to Get
- Oak's Parcel
- Earth Badge
- TM 27 (Fissure)

Any Pokémon?
- Fish for Poliwag and Goldeen once you get a Fishing Rod!

Route 2

This tree-lined path takes you to Pewter City via Viridian Forest. There's not much to see or do here—except capture some Bug Pokémon—until you've learned the skill Cut from HM 01. Then you can cut down the little bushes and explore the right side of the road!

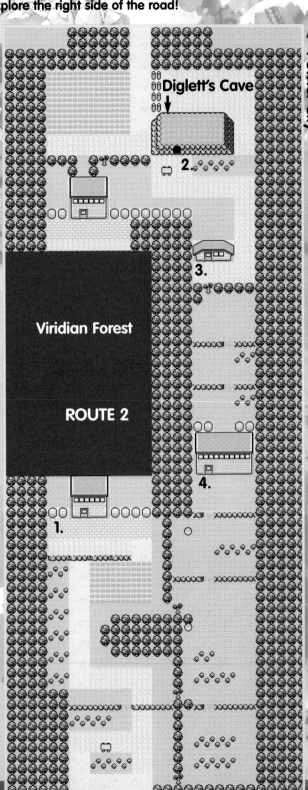

Diglett's Cave

Pewter City

Viridian Forest

ROUTE 2

2.

3.

4.

1.

Viridian City

14

1. Entrance to Viridian Forest

This little building leads into Viridian Forest. The people there will tell you a little bit about what to expect, but that's all. Make sure that you've stocked up on Antidote and Poké Balls before you enter. Healing your crew at the Viridian City Pokémon Center first is also a good idea.

2. Diglett's Cave

Until one of your Pokémon learns how to Fly with HM 02, you'll have to rely on Diglett's Cave to take you from the area east of Mt. Moon back to here. With the Cut skill, you'll be able to slice down the saplings blocking the path and go home for a quick visit!

3. Trader Alert!

The person inside this house is willing to trade you his Mr. Mime for your Abra. If you don't have one yet, write a note to yourself to come back when you do!

4. An Illuminating Visit

The people in this building are full of good information about Hidden Machine 05 and its skill Flash. Apparently Pokémon with this skill can light up whole dungeons. If you've captured 10 Pokémon by the time you reach this building, they'll give you your own copy of HM 05.

Note

There are five Hidden Machines hidden in the world of Pokémon that you must find and use if you want to complete your journey. These skill machines differ from Technical Machines in that they are reusable and the skills they contain can be used in battle or while you're traveling on the Field Map. That is, once you've gotten the appropriate Badge. One warning though—once a Pokémon uses a Hidden Machine, he can never unlearn the skill it contains.

Route 2

Things to Do
- Trade an Abra for a Mr. Mime.
- Get HM 05.

Things to Get
- HM 05 (Flash)
- HP Up
- Moon Stone

Any Pokémon?

	Red	Blue
Pidgey	Common	Common
Rattata	Common	Common
Weedle	Rare	—
Caterpie	—	Rare

Viridian Forest

Viridian Forest is the first place you'll run into the bands of roadside Trainers that will haunt you for the rest of this game. These people like to position themselves by roads or in dungeons and challenge other, unsuspecting Pokémon Trainers. Be on the lookout!

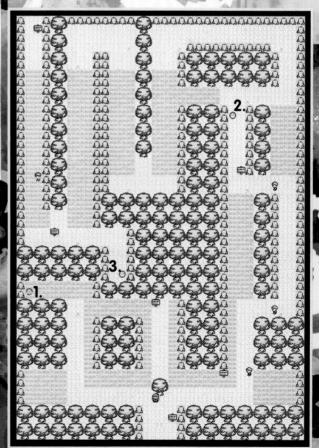

Trainer's Talk

You have three Trainers to deal with here in Viridian Forest, hidden amongst the labyrinth of trees. The three of them will try to attack you with Weedle, Caterpie, and a Kakuna between the levels of 6 and 9. The Kakuna will be the easiest to take out since he can only cast the skill Harden on himself. Try to use a Fire Pokémon like the Charmander or Flight Pokémon like Spearow or Pidgey against them for the best results.

Note

Calling all Pikachu fans. Here's your chance to finally own a Pikachu! You won't find one very often in these woods, but when you do you should try to capture it. Electric Pokémon like Pikachu are great against both Water and Flight Pokémon and make great companions for Charmanders and Squirtles.

Viridian Forest

Things to Get

1. Poké Ball
2. Antidote
3. Potion

Any Pokémon?

	Red	Blue
Weedle	Common	Rare
Kakuna	Common	Rare
Caterpie	Rare	Common
Metapod	Rare	Common
Pikachu	Rare	Rare

Pewter City

Defeating Pewter City's boss is integral to continuing your quest. A sentry from the Gym won't let you enter Route 3 until you've defeated Brock! While you're in town be sure to visit the Museum. They have an exhibit of ancient Pokémon going on that you've got to see.

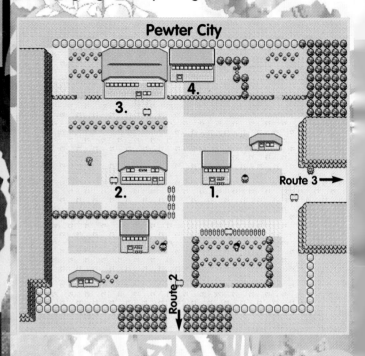

Pewter City

1. Visit the Poké Mart

Before facing Brock or heading down Route 3 to explore Mt. Moon, be sure to buy some Potions here first.

Merchandise	
Poké Ball	200P
Potion	300P
Escape Rope	550P
Antidote	100P
Burn Heal	250P
Awakening	200P
Parlyz Heal	200P

2. Fight at the Gym!

Are you ready for your first bout with a Gym Leader? From the looks of the pillars at the entrance, it appears that your Rival has already been here and gone.

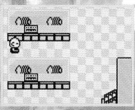
3. The Pewter Museum of Science

This month's exhibit features the remains of ancient Pokémon. Judging from the skeletons, those monsters were pretty fierce. Go ahead and spend the 50P to get in; it's worth it.

4. Wonder What They're Researching In There?

On the research side of the Museum, which you can enter once you've learned the Cut ability, the paleontologists are full of stories about fossils being brought to life. And if that's not enough, someone's found a fossil of an Aerodactyl. Maybe they'll let you borrow it?

Gym Leader Lowdown #1: Brock of the Pewter City Gym

The time has finally come to face your first Gym Leader, and he's going to toss you a curve! Up to now, you've only fought tiny Bug, Bird, and Rodent Pokémon and I'll bet they've been pretty easy to defeat. Well, that's about to change. Brock's Gym is devoted to the art of raising Rock and Ground Pokémon. These chunks of stone and precious gems are hard to defeat unless you have a powerful Water or Grass Pokémon on your side. If you chose the Charmander at the start, make sure that he's a well-seasoned warrior, accompanied by a Bug Pokémon that can help out if assistance is needed.

When you win, Brock will surrender the Boulder Badge and TM 34 as a reward. The Boulder Badge provides a boost to your Pokémon's attack strength and allows you to use the hidden skill Flash anywhere you'd like. TM 34 contains the skill Bide, which will be very familiar to you by the end of your battle with Brock's Onix.

Brock's Pokémon Lineup

Geodude	LV12
Onix	LV14

Note

Consider the Junior Trainers in each Gym a warm-up for the big battle with the leader. The Pokémon they use are of similar types and levels to what the big boss will use against you. Blowing through the Junior Trainers is usually a good sign that you're ready to go up against the Leader.

Pewter City

Things to Do
- Defeat Brock at the Gym.
- Get the Old Amber from the Museum's research facility.

Places to Go
- Pokémon Center
- Poké Mart
- Pewter City Gym
- Pewter Museum of Science
- Museum Research Facility

Things to Get
- Boulder Badge
- TM 34
- Old Amber

Any Pokémon?
- None

Route 3

After that fierce battle with Brock, it's time to relax in a few friendly bouts with the Trainers on this road. Then, head over to Mt. Moon and get ready to do some spelunking!

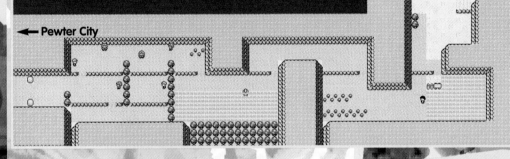

ROUTE 3

Mt. Moon

1.

← Pewter City

1. You Want To Sell Me What?

At the Pokémon Center outside of Mt. Moon, there's a man selling Magikarp for 500P. He'll make it sound like a good deal, but don't be fooled. Magikarp are not worth that much (until they become Gyrados), and you can catch them with a fishing pole almost anywhere. Save your money and wait until you get to Vermilion City!

Trainer's Talk

Along Route 3 you'll have to combat eight Trainers. This time, the Bug Catchers are back and they've brought with them stronger Caterpies and Weedles, along with a couple of Kakunas and Metapods. In addition to the Bug Catchers, you'll also run into several Youngsters and Lasses. These Trainers carry common Pokémon that you've seen and captured before or will be able to very soon. All of the Pokémon featured on this route range from LV 9 to LV 14. Your best bet is to be sensible and head back to the Pewter City Pokémon Center after every second or third battle. This is easier and, more importantly, less expensive than relying on Potions and Antidotes alone. You have a big dungeon coming up ahead, so you'll want to conserve your money for the Poké Balls and Potions you'll need while you're there.

Note

Before journeying into Mt. Moon, be sure to search the long grass for a Jigglypuff. These cute little balls of fluff and big eyes are extremely rare and can't be found in the wild anywhere else! If you're into magical and mysterious Pokémon, make this a part of your collection without fail.

Route 3

Things to Get
👁 None

Any Pokémon?

	Red	Blue
Pidgey	Common	Common
Spearow	Common	Common
Jigglypuff	Rare	Rare

Mt. Moon

Team Rocket has infiltrated Mt. Moon, and it would seem that they're up to no good. There are rumors that they've even been stealing rare fossils from the dig going on at the bottom level of the cave. Maybe you'd better go find out what they're up to.

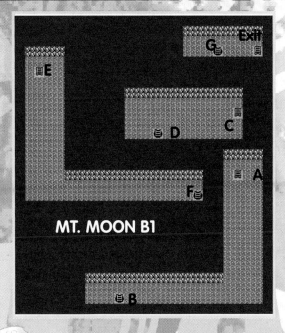

MT. MOON B1

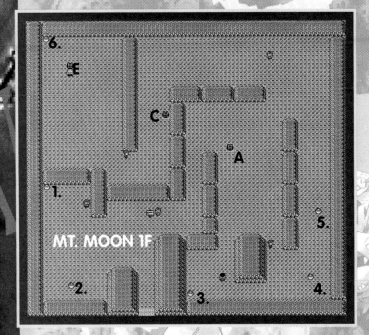

MT. MOON 1F

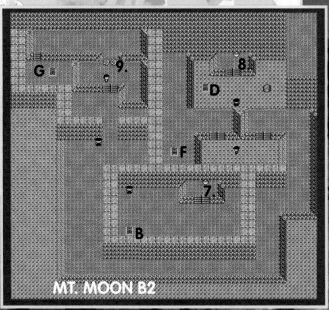

MT. MOON B2

Trainer's Talk

Much like Route 3, the first floor is filled with Youngsters, Bug Catchers, and Lasses. Their motley assortment of Pokémon have grown somewhat and are now between levels 10 and 11. New Pokémon to look out for include a LV 14 Clefairy, an Oddish and Bellsprout duo, and a Super Nerd's pet Magnemite and Voltorb. Expect to battle seven of them before you've cleared the floor. And, as with Route 3, save your Potions and make good use of the Pokémon Center right outside.

Floor B2 is filled with Team Rocket members. These bullies are known for their evil crimes and the way they mistreat Pokémon. The Rockets in Mt. Moon fight with a variety of Normal, Ground, and even Poisonous Pokémon. There are five of them lurking on this floor.

Decisions, Decisions

When you reach the end of Floor B2, you'll find a Super Nerd guarding his find of two rare fossils. If you defeat him, he'll let you choose one of them. The Dome Fossil represents the lost species of Kabuto while the Helix Fossil carries the DNA of the Omanyte. Regardless of which you choose, put it in a safe place and don't lose it!

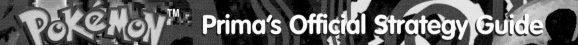

Mt. Moon

Things to Get
1. Potion
2. TM 12 (Water Gun)
3. Potion
4. Rare Candy
5. Escape Rope
6. Moon Stone
7. HP Up
8. TM 01 (Mega Punch)
9. Dome Fossil or Helix Fossil

Any Pokémon?

	Red	Blue
Zubat	Common	Common
Geodude	Rare	Rare
Paras	Rare	Rare
Clefairy	Rare	Rare

Route 4

Once you leave Mt. Moon and enter the patch of long grass to the west, you'll find that you can't get back to Mt. Moon or the cities before it. Don't be concerned, since Cerulean City is where you want to go. There are no Trainers to be found here, but you can pick up TM 04 (Whirlwind) on the second set of plateaus. You'll also want to scour the grass land for your first unique Pokémon—the Sandshrew for those of you with the Blue version and the Ekans for the Red version.

Route 4

Things to Get
1. TM 04 (Whirlwind)

Any Pokémon?

	Red	Blue
Rattata	Common	Common
Spearow	Rare	Rare
Ekans	Rare	—
Sandshrew	—	Rare

Mt. Moon

1.

ROUTE 4

Cerulean City →

Cerulean City

Your passage out of Cerulean City is blocked until you accomplish a few things. First you have to defeat Misty at the Cerulean City Gym. Then take a stroll over Nugget Bridge to visit that Pokémaniac, Bill, whom everyone's raving about. If you can help him out of a predicament, he'll reward you handsomely. Once you've done that, your path out of the city will be cleared … sort of.

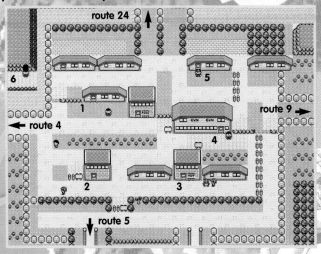

Merchandise

Poké Ball	200P
Potion	200P
Repel	350P
Antidote	100P
Burn Heal	250P
Awakening	200P
Parlyz Heal	200P

4. Cerulean City Gym

If you didn't know that Misty and her friends were totally into Water Pokémon, you'd almost think this Gym was flooded. Don't think for a minute that you'll be able to avoid the Junior Trainer swimming in the water! The moment that Swimmer sees you, he'll rush right over to the dock you're standing on.

1. Trader Alert!

There's a guy over here who wants to trade a rare Jynx for a common Poliwhirl. Can you believe it? If I were you, I'd file this away and when you get a good Fishing Rod, use it to catch one for him!

2. What an Expensive Bike!

Who ever heard of spending a 1,000,000P for a bicycle? A kid like you will never be able to afford that. Wonder if they ever go on sale …?

3. Shopping, Anyone?

Here's a list of the wares you can purchase in Cerulean City. If battling Wild Pokémon is starting to become a pain, try out some of that Repel spray. I hear it works wonders.

5. What's a Rocket Doing Here?

Team Rocket is up to its old tricks again! This time it's raiding houses and stealing TMs. The owner of this house is distraught about the loss of his new Dig TM. Now he'll have to teach his Diglett the trick himself. Maybe the guy behind the house knows something about it?

6. The Unknown Dungeon

You're dying to know how you get there, aren't you? Well, you'll have to wait until you get HM 03 and the Surf ability. Then go to the other side of Nugget Bridge and surf around to the entrance. The catch? You have to be a member of the Pokémon League before you can enter, which means beating the Elite Four at Indigo Plateau first.

Gym Leader Lowdown #2: Misty of the Cerulean City Gym

She's cute, she's bubbly, and she always wears a bathing suit. She's Misty, and she raises Pokémon of the Water variety! If you haven't already experienced this with the Squirtle, a strong Electric or Grass Pokémon is a Water type's worst enemy. Having a Pikachu, Bulbasaur/Ivysaur, or Paras on hand will make this bout go by quickly. If not, make sure that your Pokémon are pretty strong to begin with, around LV 25.

Defeating Misty earns you the Cascade Badge. This one makes all Pokémon up to LV 30 obey you without fail. This will come as a big relief to those of you with traded Pokémon who are misbehaving badly (as long as they're below LV 30). The Cascade Badge also makes it possible for you to use the Cut skill (HM 01) out in the field. In addition to the Cascade Badge you also earn TM 11, which teaches any Water Pokémon the skill Bubble Beam. If you have a Squirtle in your party, this skill makes a great addition to his repertoire.

Misty's Pokémon Lineup
Staryu   LV18
Starmie LV21

Cerulean City

Things to Do
- ◉ Defeat Misty at the Gym.
- ◉ Visit Bill's house on Route 25.
- ◉ Defeat the Team Rocket Member behind the burgled house.
- ◉ Trade a Poliwhirl for a Jynx.
- ◉ Obtain a Bicycle.

Places to Go
- ◉ Pokémon Center
- ◉ Poké Mart
- ◉ Cerulean City Gym
- ◉ Trader's House
- ◉ Burgled House

Things to Get
- ◉ Cascade Badge
- ◉ TM 11 (Bubble Beam)
- ◉ TM 28 (Dig)

Any Pokémon?
- ◉ Try fishing in the Gym for Goldeen, Krabby, and Psyduck.

Routes 24 and 25

To reach Bill's house, you'll first have to defeat the 17 other Trainers blocking your path. The first one to come along is none other than your Rival. Now he's up to four Pokémon, including his starting monster, a LV 18 Pidgeotto and a LV 15 Abra. Hopefully you've been keeping up with him!

ROUTES 24 & 25

Nugget Bridge

Once you've defeated your Rival, a Team Rocket Member will challenge you to a duel. Defeat all five of his friends and he'll give you a Nugget as a reward. The hardest of these five Trainers will be the final one, who will attack with a LV 18 Mankey. Because you can return to town and the Pokémon Center at any time during this challenge, it might be a good idea to face this Trainer fully healed. Don't think that number five will be the final Trainer you face here. The Rocket isn't happy that you won and will try to compel you to join his organization with force.

The Practice Area

Right after you've completed the Nugget Bridge challenge you'll face another group of Trainers. The Hikers in this group rely mostly on Ground and Rock Pokémon like Geodude, Machop, and Onix. Be prepared and hit them with a Pokémon using the Bubble Beam skill that you won from Misty. A Pokémon equipped with the Mega Punch skill found in Mt. Moon will also survive against these tough creatures.

Bill's House

The rumors about Bill were right; he is a Pokémaniac. He's even turned himself into a Pokémon! Help him out by starting up the transformer machine in his house. Then, once he's back to his regular self, he'll give you a ticket to the Trainers' Party on the S.S. Anne. Don't forget to visit him a second time to check out his files on rare Pokémon. He has some interesting information about a monster called Eevee.

Routes 24 & 25

Things to Get
1. Nugget
2. TM 45 (Thunderwave)
3. TM 19 (Seismic Toss)
4. S.S. Ticket (from Bill)

Any Pokémon?

	Red	Blue
Weedle	Common	Rare
Kakuna	Common	Rare
Caterpie	Rare	Common
Metapod	Rare	Common
Oddish	Rare	—
Bellsprout	—	Rare
Abra	Rare	Rare
Pidgey	Rare	Rare

◉ Fish for Psyduck, Krabby, and Goldeen.

Route 5

When you leave Cerulean City through the Burgled House, you'll find that you can't get back in the conventional way until you've found either HM 01 (Cut) or HM 02 (Fly). You can, however, get in through the rock wall on the side of the gym. Head south to the end of the road where you'll find a gatehouse and a small building.

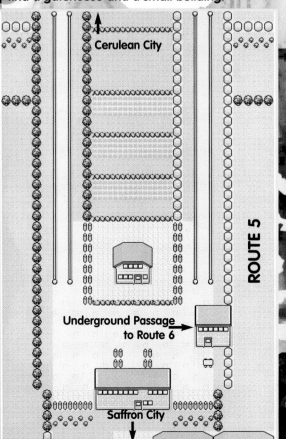

Cerulean City

Underground Passage to Route 6

ROUTE 5

Saffron City

Daycare for Pokémon

If you journey down the field between the two roads, you'll be able to enter a place called the Daycare Center. Here you can leave one of your Pokémon in the care of an expert babysitter. For a small fee, this kind soul will raise your Pokémon for you. Just don't forget to pick it up sometime!

Thirsty Guards

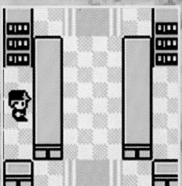

There's a city closer to you than you realize. Unfortunately the roads are under construction and the gatehouse guards are feeling a little bit grouchy because they're really thirsty. Maybe they'd let you pass if you could find them some water or a Soda Pop.

Underground Path

Don't let the closed roads scare you. There are other ways to get around this area. In the house to the right of the gatehouse is the entrance to an Underground Path. This tunnel will take you from Route 5 to Route 6 in no time flat. And you won't even have to fight any monsters on the way.

Route 6

Now that you've made it through the Underground Path, you only need to walk south to Vermilion City. As you go, check the tall grass for rare and unique species of Pokémon.

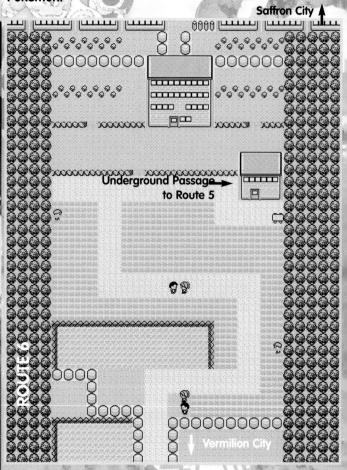

Saffron City ↑

Underground Passage → to Route 5

ROUTE 6

↓ Vermilion City

Trainer's Talk

You'll find Bug Catchers and Junior Trainers alike in this grassy meadow. The most difficult battle will be against a LV 20 Butterfree that has nasty sleep spells. Be sure to stock up on Awakening before you come here.

Route 5

Things to Get
👁 None

Any Pokémon?

	Red	Blue
Pidgey	Common	Common
Oddish	Rare	—
Mankey	Rare	—
Bellsprout	—	Rare
Meowth	—	Rare

Route 6

Things to Get
👁 None

Any Pokémon?

	Red	Blue
Pidgey	Common	Common
Oddish	Rare	—
Mankey	Rare	—
Bellsprout	—	Rare
Meowth	—	Rare

Vermilion City

Welcome to the seaside city of Vermilion. Here Pokémon and Pokémaniacs are celebrated by all. If you don't believe me, pay a visit to the Pokémon Fan Club!

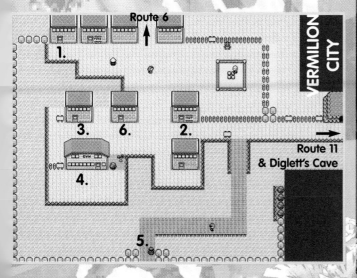

Route 6

VERMILION CITY

Route 11 & Diglett's Cave

1. Hand-Me-Down Fishing Poles

The Fishing Guru of Vermilion City is willing to give you his old Fishing Rod. So what if it doesn't work very well? You can still catch plenty of Magikarp with it. Besides, this guy has two brothers who are also handing out poles.

2. Vermilion City Poké Mart

Here's the list of merchandise that the Poké Mart sells. You ought to try their Super Potion before you head over to the S.S. Anne.

Merchandise	
Poké Ball	200P
Super Potion	700P
Ice Heal	250P
Awakening	200P
Parlyz Heal	200P
Repel	350P

3. Pokémon Fans Unite!

The president of the Pokémon Fan Club loves to talk about his rare Pokémon. Did you know that his favorite is the Rapidash? Hear him out and he'll give you his Bike Voucher, good for this year's bike over at the Cerulean City Bicycle Shop.

4. An Electric Gym

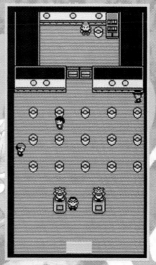

Before you can enter the Vermilion City Gym, you must have gotten the Cut ability (HM 01) from the Captain of the S.S. Anne. Then you'll have to figure out the code to unlock the door to Lt. Surge's room. Defeat the Junior Trainers and make them talk.

5. A Party on the S.S. Anne

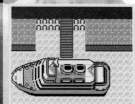

Before you can do much of anything in this city, like take on its Trainer, you'll need to visit the Captain on the S.S. Anne.

6. Trader Alert!

This one is easy. A trader is willing to give up his rare FarFetch'd for a very common Spearow. Surely you have one of those in your collection.

Gym Leader Lowdown #3: Lt. Surge of the Viridian City Gym

Before you can challenge Lt. Surge, you have to undo the electrical lock that he's used to keep people out. The Trainers will talk—once you've beaten them—and tell you its secret. You have to look in the garbage bins and when you find the first lock, the second will be in a neighboring can.

Lt. Surge is the leader of an order of Pokémon Trainers dedicated to Electric Pokémon. Only Ground Pokémon have a special affinity for defeating Electric Pokémon, so if you were able to pick one up during your travels, you might want to equip him with the Dig skill you picked up before leaving Cerulean City.

When you defeat Lt. Surge, you'll receive the Thunder Badge. This Badge allows you to use the hidden skill Fly in and out of battle. It also ups all of your Pokémon's speed. In addition to the Badge, Lt. Surge will also give you his TM 24. This teaches the skill Thunderbolt and is a handy addition to any Electric Pokémon.

Lt. Surge's Pokémon Lineup

Voltorb LV 21
Pikachu LV 18
Raichu   LV 24

Vermilion City

Things to Do
- Get HM 01 (Cut) from the Captain of the S.S. Anne.
- Defeat Lt. Surge at the Gym.
- Talk to the President of the Pokémon Fan Club.
- Trade a Spearow for a FarFetch'd.
- Get the Old Rod from the Fishing Guru.

Places to Go
- Pokémon Center
- Poké Mart
- Viridian City Gym
- Trader's House
- Pokémon Fan Club
- Fishing Guru's House

Things to Get
- Bike Voucher
- Old Rod
- Thunder Badge
- TM 24

Any Pokémon?
- Try fishing in the Gym for Krabby and Shelder.

S.S. Anne

This cruise ship is filled with Trainers waiting for a good challenge. As you wander through the decks of this luxury ship, you have the opportunity to talk to the passengers resting in their staterooms. Beware, some will want to fight you, while others will just dispense good advice.

S.S. Anne—Main Deck

Mess Hall

S.S. Anne—Lower Deck

Captain's Room

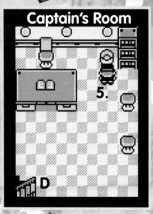

5.

D

Mess Hall

2

S.S. Anne—Upper Deck

A   B   4   D

C

S.S. Anne—Bow

C

Trainer's Talk

The gang of Trainers on the S.S. Anne are a motley bunch ranging from distinguished Gentlemen and Lasses to coarse Fishermen and Sailors. Their Pokémon are also a mixed bag, but you can count on one thing: when you battle a Fisherman or Sailor, you can expect to see a lot of Water Pokémon. All of them fall within the LV 17 to LV 23 range of experience levels.

What's a Party Without Good Friends?

Well, I wouldn't exactly call your Rival a good friend, but he's here on the S.S. Anne. Use this battle to check your own progress. If you beat him easily, then you're doing a great job!

"Do You Have Anything for Seasickness?"

The Captain is suffering from a dangerous bout of seasickness. When you help him out, he'll give you your first Hidden Machine. This one teaches the valuable skill Cut, which allows you to cut down the small trees blocking parts of the path. With this skill, you'll be able to get into the Viridian City Gym and back into Cerulean City.

Note

Once the Captain has regained his sea legs, it's time to set sail. Leave the boat for any reason, and it will take off without you. If you want to fight all of the Trainers and pick up all of the loot lying around, make sure that you save your trip to the Captain's chambers until the end. This way you can fight and then run out to the Pokémon Center for some healing as often as you'd like.

Route 11

Tackle this route after you've finished your business in Vermilion City and the S.S. Anne. Unfortunately, you won't be able to continue on to Route 12 since the road is blocked by a snoozing Snorlax. If only you could wake it up. Do, however, climb to the top of the gatehouse and meet with Prof. Oak's Aide. You can count on him to have a great item for you if you meet his high standards.

Route 11

Things to Get
1. TM 08 (Body Slam)
2. Great Ball
3. Max Ether
4. Rare Candy
5. HM 01
6. TM 44 (Rest)
7. Ether
8. Max Potion

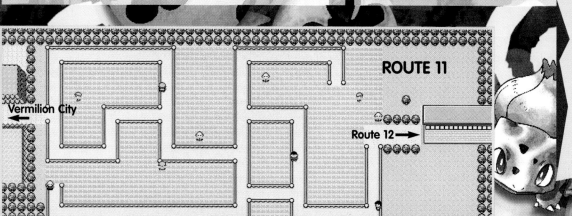

ROUTE 11

← Vermilion City

Route 12 →

Trainer's Talk

This field is full of Trainers (10 to be exact) divided between Youngsters, Gamblers, and Engineers. Of the three, the Engineers are the most predictable with their electrified Pokémon. The weakest Pokémon you'll fight here is LV 18, while the highest are at LV 21.

Itemfinder

Once you've collected 30 Pokémon, Prof. Oak's Aide will give you a special item called an Itemfinder. Use this tool to locate hidden items. If the Itemfinder locates an item, you will find it on somewhere on that screen. Use it in areas like the Underground Paths or in blocked off areas that appear to have nothing in them.

Diglett's Cave

With the Snorlax blocking the road, you won't have any other choice but to take Diglett's Cave to the other side of the continent. This long and twisting tunnel, home to many Digletts and the odd Dugtrio, is a famous shortcut between Vermilion City and Route 2 near Pewter City.

Route 11

Things to Get
1. Itemfinder

Any Pokémon?

	Red	Blue
Spearow	Common	Common
Arbok	Common	—
Sandshrew	—	Common
Drowzee	Rare	Rare

Route 9

Now that you have the Cut ability, you can take this route to Rock Tunnel and Lavender Town. The Trainers here are at about the same level as those on the S.S. Anne and Route 11, so you should have an easy time with them. If you find that your Pokémon are running short of steam, however, there is a Pokémon Center located right outside the entrance to Rock Tunnel.

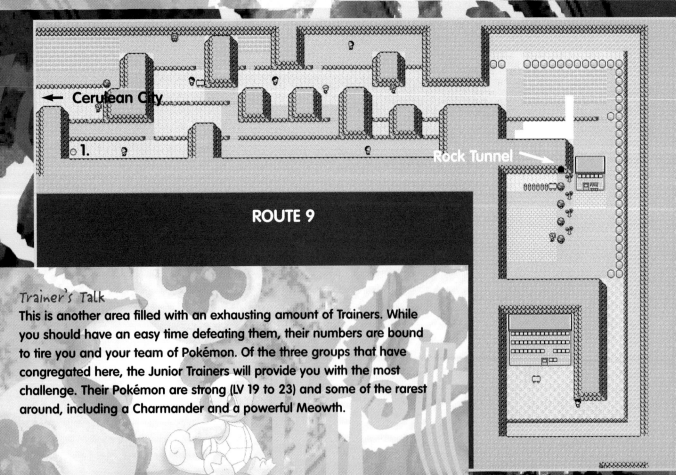

← Cerulean City

1.

Rock Tunnel →

ROUTE 9

Trainer's Talk

This is another area filled with an exhausting amount of Trainers. While you should have an easy time defeating them, their numbers are bound to tire you and your team of Pokémon. Of the three groups that have congregated here, the Junior Trainers will provide you with the most challenge. Their Pokémon are strong (LV 19 to 23) and some of the rarest around, including a Charmander and a powerful Meowth.

A Lovely Stream

When you get the Surf ability (HM 03), you'll want to come back here and explore the stream north of the Pokémon Center. An abandoned Power Plant that is inhabited by tons of Electric Pokémon is said to lie downstream. If you've been looking longingly for a Magnemite of your own, maybe this is the place to try.

Rock Tunnel

Make good use of the Pokémon Center west of the tunnel's opening. You have no idea of what lies inside, and the trek to the other side is long and treacherous.

Route 9

Things to Get
1. TM 30

Any Pokémon?

	Red	Blue
Rattata	Common	Common
Spearow	Common	Common
Arbok	Common	—
Sandshrew	—	Common
Voltorb	Common	Common

Rock Tunnel

The Rock Tunnel is a horrible place to visit if you don't have a lantern. Hopefully, you've acquired HM 05 and the Flash skill. Use it to illuminate the dark cavern inside and help you find your way through.

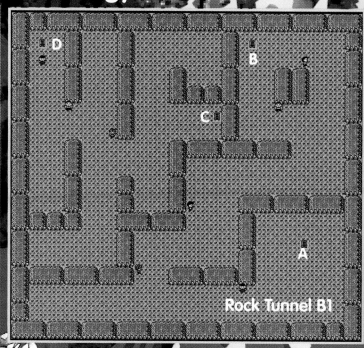

Rock Tunnel B1

Trainer's Talk

As you would expect, the Rock Tunnel is full of Rock Pokémon and Trainers carrying Rock Pokémon. Keep an eye out for Hikers with their armies of Geodudes and Onix. In addition to the Hikers, you'll also find Pokémaniacs who are desperate to show off their collections of Slowpoke and Cubones.

The Pokémon Trainers here have Pokémon that range in experience from LV 19 to LV 25.

It Sure Is Dark in Here!

You can still make it through without the Flash skill, it's just a lot harder. The walls are slightly illuminated, which will help you find your way around somewhat. Dodging Trainers in the dark will be very tricky.

Things to Get
◉ None

Any Pokémon?

	Red	Blue
Zubat	Common	Common
Geodude	Rare	Rare
Machop	Rare	Rare
Onix	Rare	Rare

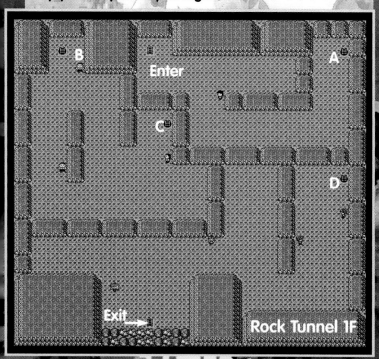

Rock Tunnel 1F

Route 10

Just when you thought it was safe to leave Rock Tunnel, you get ambushed by four Trainers. If you're seriously hurting, take the path to the right and heal yourself in Lavender Town before taking on the rest of them.

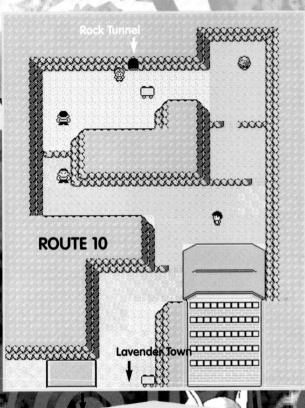

Rock Tunnel

ROUTE 10

Lavender Town

Route 10

Things to Get

◉ None

Any Pokémon?

	Red	Blue
Rattata	Common	Common
Spearow	Common	Common
Arbok	Common	—
Sandshrew	—	Common
Voltorb	Common	Common

Lavender Town

This tiny town south of the Rock Tunnel is home to the Pokémon Tower, a place where dead Pokémon are laid to rest. Right now, though, the town is buzzing about the recent hauntings there. Maybe there's something you can do to help out.

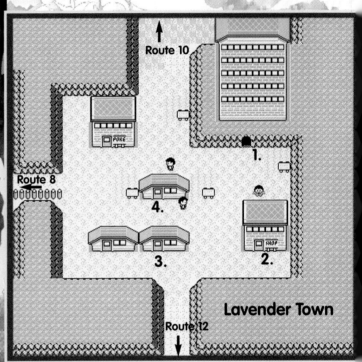

Route 10

Route 8

1.

4.

3.

2.

Lavender Town

Route 12

1. A Gastly Building

The first floor of this tall tower is perhaps the safest of them all. It appears that Team Rocket has been abusing Pokémon (especially the Cubone) and it has disrupted the spirits. You can try to climb to the top, but without a Silph Scope you won't be able to determine who is the cause of all this mayhem.

2. Any New Stuff to Buy?

The Lavender City Poké Mart is the first place you'll find the magic medicine, Revive. Having this in your inventory will help you out of a jam, if you should lose a Pokémon in battle.

Merchandise

Great Ball	600P
Super Potion	700P
Revive	1,500P
Escape Rope	550P
Super Repel	500P
Antidote	100P
Burn Heal	250P
Ice Heal	250P
Paralyze Heal	200P

3. Home of the Name Rater

If you need to change the name of one of your Pokémon (like, when your Nidoran, Fred, suddenly turns into a Nidorina), then this is the place you need to visit. The Name Rater is more than happy to help you fix your name woes.

4. Community Service

Mr. Fuji's Abandoned Pokémon House is a community-run service headed by the delightful Mr. Fuji. Unfortunately, he's being held at the top of the Pokémon Tower. If you help him out, he might surrender his most prized possession to you.

Lavender Town

Things to Do
- Free the restless ghost using the Silph Scope.
- Rescue Mr. Fuji and get the Poké Flute.

Places to Go
- Pokémon Center
- Poké Mart
- Name Rater
- Pokémon Tower
- Mr. Fuji's Abandoned Pokémon House

Things to Get
- Poké Flute

Any Pokémon?
- None

Route 8

This is the third path you've traveled that is blocked by the threat of road construction. Fortunately there's another Underground Path that you can take under Saffron City and over to Route 7. There's supposed to be a giant Department Store in nearby Celadon City that is worth checking out!

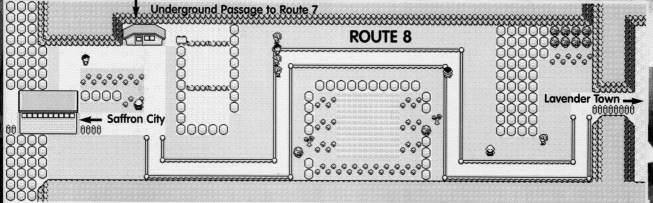

Underground Passage to Route 7

ROUTE 8

← Saffron City

Lavender Town →

Trainer's Talk

The nine Trainers here will provide you with a much needed experience boost before you enter Celadon City. The road is split between Lasses, Super Nerds, and Gamblers. Super Nerds like to use Poisonous and Electric Pokémon in battle. You won't see any cute monsters (they leave that to the Lasses), but a lot of toxic pollutants like Koffing and Muk. All of the Pokémon you deal with here are between the levels of 22 and 26.

Underground Path (E-W)

The house to the north of the gatehouse to Saffron City provides an entrance to the east-west Underground Path. Like the one you took between Cerulean City and Vermilion, this path also offers battle-free passage beneath Saffron City to the road on the other side.

Route 7

There's not much here except a plot of land that's rumored to be home to a variety of rare and unique Pokémon. Take the road to the northwest and you'll end up in Celadon City.

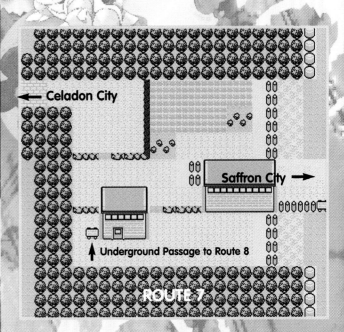

← Celadon City

Saffron City →

↑ Underground Passage to Route 8

ROUTE 7

Route 8

Things to Get
◉ None

Any Pokémon?

	Red	Blue
Pidgey	Common	Common
Mankey	Rare	—
Arbok	Rare	—
Growlithe	Rare	—
Meowth	—	Rare
Sandshrew	—	Rare
Vulpix	—	Rare

Route 7

Things to Get
◉ None

Any Pokémon?

	Red	Blue
Pidgey	Common	Common
Oddish	Rare	—
Mankey	Rare	—
Growlithe	Rare	—
Bellsprout	—	Rare
Meowth	—	Rare
Vulpix	—	Rare

Celadon City

Celadon is known for its large Department Store and Game Corner. There are rumors that the Game Corner is actually run by Team Rocket and that their Hideout is somewhere nearby. While you're in town, why don't you mix business with pleasure and pay them a visit?

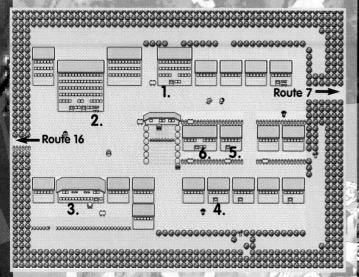

← Route 16

Route 7 →

1.
2.
3.
4.
5.
6.

1. A Rare Opportunity

There's a secret doorway into Celadon Mansion that you shouldn't miss. At the top of the staircase you'll find a solitary room with a Poké Ball inside. Inside that is a very rare Pokémon indeed, an Eevee. For more information about these creatures, pay Bill the Pokémaniac another visit.

2. The Department Store

The Celadon Department Store is a place where you can find tons of treasure. Here you can buy many items that aren't available anywhere else. When you see what's here, in conjunction with the things you can win at the Coin Exchange, you'll feel like you're in a shopper's paradise!

Merchandise—Second Floor

Great Ball	600P
Super Potion	700P
Revive	1,500P
Super Repel	500P
Antidote	100P
Burn Heal	250P
Ice Heal	250P
Awakening	200P
Parlyz Heal	200P
TM 01 (Mega Punch)	3,000P
TM 02 (Razor Wind)	2,000P
TM 05 (Mega Kick)	3,000P
TM 07 (Horn Drill)	2,000P
TM 09 (Take Down)	3,000P
TM 17 (Submission)	3,000P
TM 32 (Double Team)	1,000P
TM 33 (Reflect)	1,000P
TM 37 (Egg Bomb)	2,000P

Merchandise—Fourth Floor

Poké Doll	1,000P
Fire Stone	2,100P
Leaf Stone	2,100P
Thunder Stone	2,100P
Water Stone	2,100P

Merchandise—Fifth Floor

Dire Hit	950P
Guard Spec.	700P
X Accuracy	650P
X Attack	500P
X Defend	550P
X Speed	350P
X Special	350P
Calcium	9,800P
Carbos	9,800P
Iron	9,800P
Protein	9,800P

Merchandise—Rooftop

Fresh Water	200P
Soda Pop	300P
Lemonade	350P

Note

Don't forget to purchase a drink for the thirsty guards. Clearing the blockades between Saffron City and the rest of the world will make traveling much easier.

3. The Gym

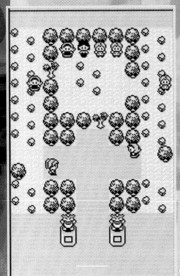

You'll have to Cut through a small tree to reach Erika's grassy Gym, and then cut through more saplings to reach Erika once inside. Don't worry—the effort will be worth it.

4. Care for a Drink?

Inside the restaurant and many houses of Celadon City, you'll see what an effect the Game Corner is having on its citizens. There's one guy in here who's ready to give up his Coin Purse, even.

5. The Coin Exchange

When you win money at the Game Corner next door, this is where you come to spend it. There's a lot of cool stuff to buy here that you can't find anywhere else!

6. A Time for Slots

Here in the Game Corner, you'll find people literally glued to their slot machines. If you talk to them, you can count on them to give you coins to go away. You can either sit down to play slots for a while or check out the back of the store. What's that Rocket doing there? Guarding a poster?

TMs Everywhere

Be sure to talk to everyone you meet in the Department Store. They're just giving TMs away there! Also Surf across the little pond in the center of town and talk to the old lady there. She'll give you a TM, too.

Gym Leader Lowdown #4: Erika of the Celadon City Gym

That Erika's a nature lover is plain to see from the look of her Gym. Surrounded by trees and her handmaidens, you'd almost think you stepped into a storybook or something. Grass Pokémon rule here and that's good for all of you Flame Pokémon carriers. Almost any Pokémon works well against these powerful plants, except for Water, Electric, and Ground types.

When you win, Erika will give you the pretty Rainbow Badge. This ups your Pokémon's attack strength and makes monsters up to LV 50 obey you without fail. The TM she gives you as a parting gift is Mega Drain, which steals HP from enemy Pokémon and gives them to you!

Erika's Pokémon Lineup

Victreebel	LV 29
Tangela	LV 24
Vileplume	LV 29

Celadon City

Things to Do
◉ Defeat Erika at the Gym.
◉ Get the Eevee from Celadon Mansion.
◉ Get the Coin Purse from the Bar.
◉ Visit the Game Corner.
◉ Shop at the Celadon Department Store.
◉ Get the Silph Scope from Team Rocket's Hideout.

Places to Go
◉ Pokémon Center
◉ Celadon Department Store
◉ Celadon Mansion
◉ Celadon City Gym
◉ Bar
◉ Game Corner
◉ Coin Exchange

Things to Get
◉ Rainbow Badge
◉ Silph Scope
◉ Coin Purse
◉ TM 13 (Ice Beam)
◉ TM 18 (Counter)
◉ TM 21 (Mega Drain)
◉ TM 41 (Softboiled)
◉ TM 48 (Rock Slide)
◉ TM 49 (Tri Attack)

Any Pokémon?
◉ Eevee
◉ Try fishing for Poliwhirl and Slowpoke.

The Game Corner and Team Rocket's Hideout
There's a suspicious Team Rocket member guarding what looks like a poster. Talk to him and you'll find him even more suspicious—especially when he attacks you. Then, once he's run away, examine the picture and pull the lever you find there.

Game Corner 1F

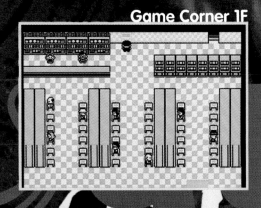

Game Corner B1 First Floor

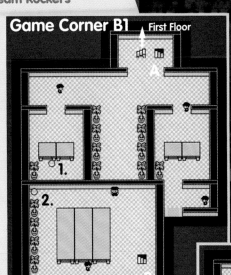

Game Corner B2

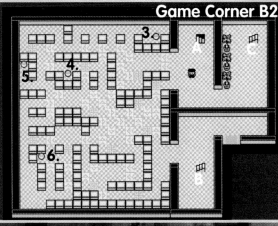

Game Corner B3

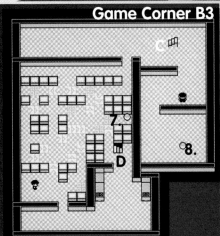

Game Corner B4

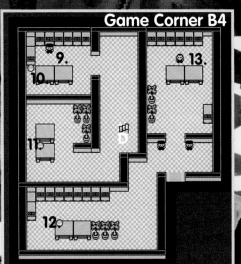

Rooms of Propulsion Pads!

Not having a Lift Key, means that you'll have to make your way through two rooms filled with tiny propulsion pads. These pads propel you unstoppably in the direction they point until you come to another propulsion pad or a stop pad. If you take a moment to figure out which way each set of pads will take you; finding the path across will be easy.

Don't Be Afraid of Roughing Them Up

Once you defeat a Team Rocket member, talk to them a second time and you'll find that they sing like birds. This is the only way that you'll find important items like the Lift Key.

The Leader of the Rockets

In an office off the Elevator you'll find the office of Team Rocket's boss. Giovanni is a busy person, but your appearance in his hideout is enough to make him stop working and pay attention. You'll have to defeat him and his collection of strong (LV 24 to LV 29) Ground and Rock monsters to make him cough up the Silph Scope.

Trainer's Talk

There's nothing but Rockets in here! As you fight your way through the Team Rocket Hideout, you'll see a lot of Poisonous Pokémon and Rattata. These guys are challenging and range in experience from LV 17 to LV 23.

The Game Corner & Team Rocket's Hideout

Things to Get

1. Escape Rope
2. Hyper Potion
3. Nugget
4. TM 07 (Horn Drill)
5. Moon Stone
6. Super Potion
7. Rare Candy
8. TM 10 (Double-Edge)
9. Lift Key
10. TM 02 (Razor Wind)
11. HP Up
12. Iron
13. Silph Scope

Pokémon Tower

With the Silph Scope in hand, its time to tackle the Pokémon Tower. And you'll need to if you want to get to Fuchsia City and the coast beyond. The Ghosts inside will seem difficult until you find out which Pokémon do best against them. Also, if you're lucky, you might run across one of the almost-extinct Cubone.

Pokémon Tower 1F

Pokémon Tower 2F

Pokémon Tower 3F

Pokémon Tower 4F

Pokémon Tower 5F

Pokémon Tower 6F

Pokémon Tower 7F

Trainer's Talk

All of the Channelers here will attack you with a Gastly and possibly a Haunter. When you add these to the numbers of wild spirits roaming around, you'll feel like a ghost expert when you're through. To get you started, Ghost Pokémon aren't extremely susceptible to anyone's attacks and they have a stunning resistance to both Normal and Fighting skills. Poison and Bug attacks don't fare too well either, but at least they inflict some damage. Your best bet is to experiment with the Pokémon and skills you have available, and decide what works best for you.

Spiritual Healing

The strange square on the Fifth Floor is there to heal your battle wounds before you go off to face the final two floors. Don't forget where it is, just in case.

And the Ghost Revealed ...

... is that of a mother Marowak, angered at the brutal death of her children. Defeating her is an act of compassion that will send her spirit to rest at last.

Pokémon Tower

Things to Get

1. Escape Rope
2. HP Up
3. Awakening
4. Elixir
5. Nugget
6. X Accuracy
7. Rare Candy

Any Pokémon?

	Red	Blue
Gastly	Common	Common
Haunter	Rare	Rare
Cubone	Rare	Rare

Saffron City

Saffron City, nestled in the heart of Pokémon country, is the largest city in the land. Home to Silph Co. headquarters, it hosts some of the finest minds in the world. Which is why it should come as no surprise to you to find Team Rocket here in full force. They've taken over the city and you won't get far unless you kick them out!

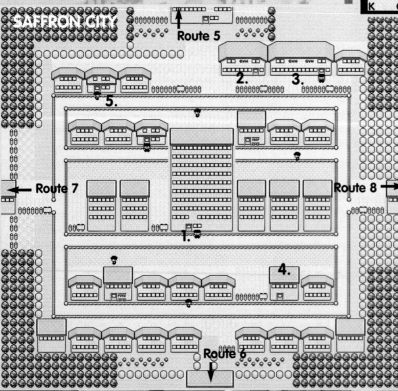

1. Silph Co.

This is the source of all of your problems right now, and you might want to take a look around here first. Sometimes it's hard to believe the lengths to which evil-doers will go.

2. The Fighting Dojo: a Splinter Gym

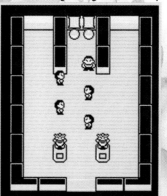

When the Saffron City Gym became too crowded and big, part of their clientele decided to open their own Gym dedicated to raising Fighting Pokémon. Now, going in there is like going into a real Gym, except that instead of a Badge you get your choice of rare Fighting Pokémon as your prize.

3. Saffron City Gym: the Original

I N	J M	F L	J K	G I	C H
E M	L O			G N	B F
H K	D O		A	C D	B A

Right next door (although inaccessible until you've cleared the Rockets out of town) is the real Gym. Home to a bunch of psychically oriented Trainers, this place is filled with teleport pads, Channelers, and real live psychics.

4. Mr. Psychic

Visit this house and Mr. Psychic will give you TM 29, which is Psychic.

5. Give the Kid a Doll

If you bring the little girl a Poké Doll from neighboring Celadon City, she'll gladly give you TM 31 (Mimic).

Gym Leader Lowdown #5: Sabrina of the Saffron City Gym

To reach Sabrina, you'll have to teleport almost throughout the entire Gym. The Trainers here (all Psychics and Channelers) are big fans of Psychic and Ghost Pokémon. Ghosts we already know are immune to Normal and Fighting attacks, and you have to get creative with them to defeat them. Psychics on the other hand are easily defeated by Bugs and their Ghostly friends. If you have either one in your possession, you might want to consider pulling it into the fray.

The Marsh Badge that you receive as a reward makes all Pokémon LV 70 and below obey your every command and TM 46 (Psywave) is sure to please one of your psychically gifted Pokémon.

Sabrina's Pokémon Lineup:

Kadabra	LV 38
Mr. Mime	LV 37
Venomoth	LV 38
Alakazam	LV 43

Saffron City

Things to Do
- 👁 Defeat the head of the Fighting Dojo.
- 👁 Rescue the President of the Silph Co. and get the Master Ball.
- 👁 Defeat Sabrina at the Saffron City Gym.

Places to Go
- 👁 Pokémon Center
- 👁 Poké Mart
- 👁 Silph Company
- 👁 Saffron City Gym
- 👁 Fighting Dojo
- 👁 Mr. Psychic
- 👁 Mimic's House

Things to Get
- 👁 Marsh Badge
- 👁 TM 29 (Psychic)
- 👁 TM 31 (Mimic)
- 👁 TM 46 (Psywave)

Any Pokémon?
- 👁 Hitmonlee or Hitmonchan

Silph Co.

In the middle of Saffron City lies the headquarters for the Silph Co. Team Rocket has taken the building over in the hopes of finding the secret to their new product, the Master Ball. They've raided their labs and even taken the company's President hostage in their quest. Help the Silph Co. and its employees!

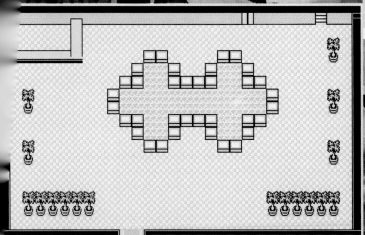

Silph Co. 1F

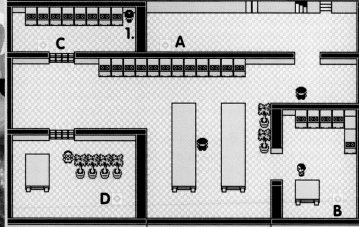

Silph Co. 2F

Silph Co. 3F

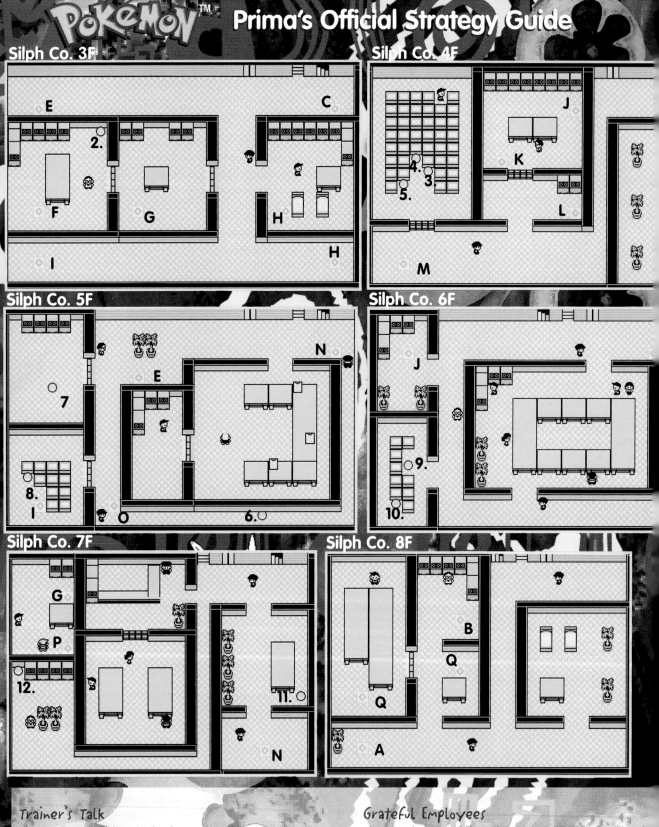

Silph Co. 4F

Silph Co. 5F

Silph Co. 6F

Silph Co. 7F

Silph Co. 8F

Trainer's Talk

This 11-floor building is the largest and most tiring dungeon of the game. There are 30 Trainers here ranging from Poison-spitting Rockets to electrical Scientists. The experience levels here start at LV 25 and go up.

Grateful Employees

The employees of the Silph Co. are scared to death not only about their jobs but their lives as well. If yo stop to talk with them and allay their fears, they mig have a helpful gift for you. Remember this before yo take the teleport pad to the President's office.

Silph Co. 9F

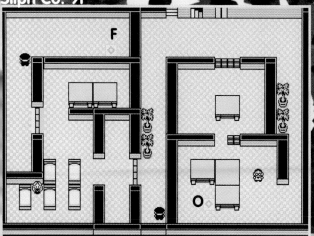

Silph Co. 10F

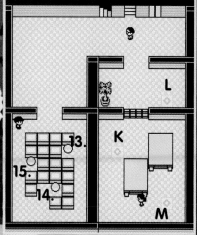

Silph Co. 11F

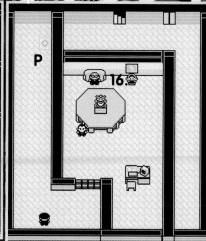

Teleport Pads and Key Cards

You will have an easier time if you get the Key Card before using the Teleport pads extensively. By the time you find this item on the Fifth Floor, you should have taken out about half of the enemy Trainers. If you clear out the rest of the levels before you start zapping around, you will have effectively taken care of any deadly situations before going up against the boss.

The Rest Ward

When you find the Silph Co. worker next to the bed, you'll know you're getting close to Giovanni, the head Rocket. Here you can rest and heal your Pokémon's wounds before going up against the boss man himself.

Didn't I Just Fight You?

Why didn't your Rival do anything to free the Silph Co.? Is he just here to taunt you? Defeat him again and then go on to the 11th Floor.

A Master Ball

To rescue the Silph Co. President you must battle with Giovanni once again. This time he's added some high-level Nidoran to his arsenal, so watch out for their poisonous attacks. With Pokémon in the LV 35 to LV 41 range, he's going to be tough to defeat. But if you found the battle against your Rival pretty easy, then this will be too. With Giovanni vanquished once again, you'll find yourself on the receiving end of a fabulous reward, the Master Ball. You only get one of these, so use it with discretion.

Note

It's highly recommended that you store the Master Ball away until you can enter the Unknown Dungeon. The Mewtwo there is fierce but a highly desirable Pokémon. Using your Master Ball on him is a very good idea!

Silph Co.

Things to Get

1. TM 36 (Self Destruct)
2. Hyper Potion
3. Escape Rope
4. Max Revive
5. Full Heal
6. Key Card
7. Protein
8. TM 09 (Take Down)
9. HP Up
10. X Accuracy
11. TM 03 (Swords Dance)
12. Calcium
13. Carbos
14. Rare Candy
15. TM 26 (Earthquake)
16. Master Ball

Any Pokémon?
◎ Lapras

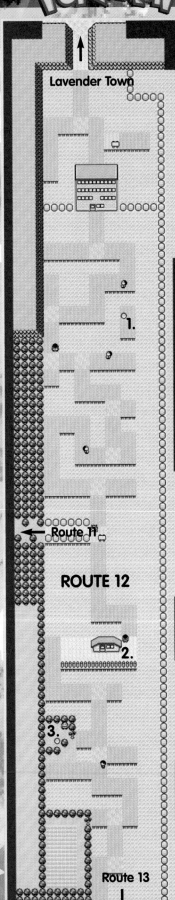

Lavender Town

1.

← Route 11

ROUTE 12

2.

3.

Route 13 ↓

Route 12

South of Lavender Town is a series of interconnected docks that span the entire eastern coast of the Pokémon realm. If you have the Surf ability, you can glide down the side with no interruptions whatsoever. If you don't, you'll have to walk and deal with the Fishermen you meet on the way.

The Snorlax In the Road

You won't make it far unless you have a Poké Flute in your possession. A big Snorlax is blocking the road and the only way to wake him is with that flute. Once awake, he'll attack and you'll have an opportunity to capture him. Try to use Ultra Balls if you've made it to Fuchsia City already. If not, I hope that you have a large supply of Super Balls on hand. This rare Pokémon is tough to catch.

What a Great Fishing Pole!

One of the Fishing Guru's brothers has bought a house on Route 12. This is a great opportunity for you to learn even more about fishing lore. If you listen closely to what this guy has to say, he'll give you a Super Rod that will allow you to catch all kinds of fish.

Route 12

Things to Get
1. TM 16
2. Super Rod
3. Iron

Any Pokémon?

	Red	Blue
Pidgey	Common	Common
Oddish	Rare	—
Gloom	Rare	—
Venonat	Rare	—
Bellsprout	—	Rare
Weepinbell	—	Rare

◉ Fish for Tentacool, Krabby, Magikarp, and Goldeen.

Route 13

The Birdkeepers here are fierce with lots of Flight Pokémon hovering around the LV 30 mark. This is a good area to build your Pokémon's experience levels. With the Fuchsia City Gym coming up and then the dungeon under the Seafoam Islands, you'll want to make sure that your Pokémon are up to the challenge.

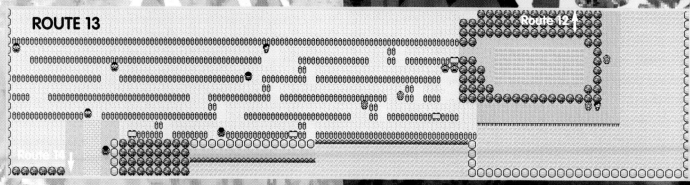

ROUTE 13

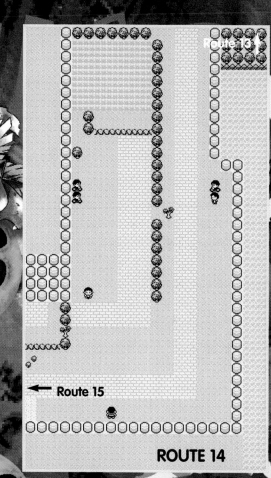

Route 13

Things to Get

👁 None

Any Pokémon?:

	Red	Blue
Pidgey	Rare	Rare
Ditto	Rare	Rare
Venonat	Rare	Rare
Oddish	Rare	—
Gloom	Rare	—
Bellsprout	—	Rare
Weepinbell	—	Rare

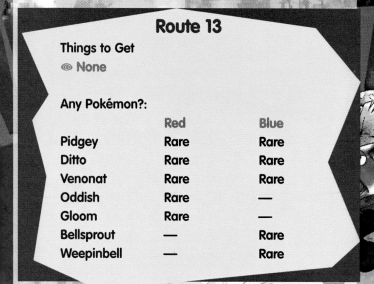

Routes 14 and 15

There are some patches of land where it's easy to capture the wild second forms of some of your favorite Pokémon. This stretch of the road is one of them. Hunt in the thickets for advanced Pokémon like the Pidgeotto, Gloom, and Weepinbell. If you haven't bothered to level up any of their first forms, this will really save you time.

ROUTE 14

ROUTE 15

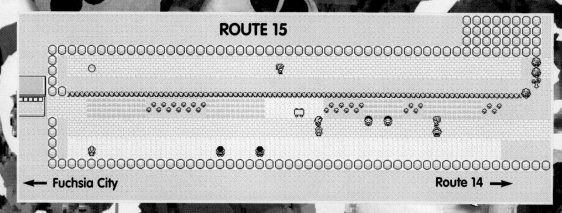

Got 50 Pokémon Yet?

If you've collected 50 Pokémon, Prof. Oak's Aide has another present for you. This time you'll get a piece of research equipment called Exp. All. When you have this amongst your Items, all of the Pokémon you have with you will receive a portion of the experience points handed out after a battle. Here's how it works: The experience points earned are divided in half first and one half is divided among all of your party. The other half is divided among the Pokémon who actually participated in battle. Sound neat? Well, when your party is small it is. But if you are carting around six Pokémon, the allotment of all of those experience points can get kind of time consuming.

Routes 14 & 15

Things to Get

- 👁 TM 20
- 👁 Exp. All

Any Pokémon?

	Red	Blue
Pidgey	Rare	Rare
Pidgeotto	Rare	Rare
Ditto	Rare	Rare
Venonat	Rare	Rare
Oddish	Rare	—
Gloom	Rare	—
Bellsprout	—	Rare
Weepinbell	—	Rare

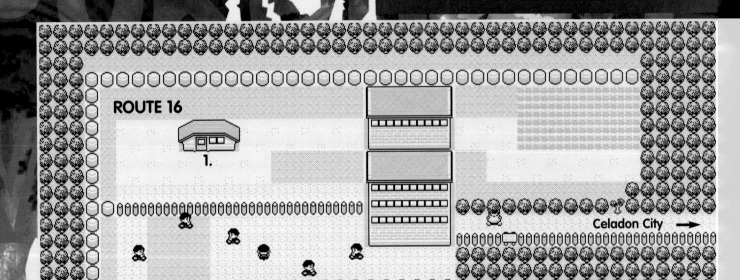

ROUTE 16

1.

Celadon City →

Route 17

Route 16

Before you can get very far down Route 16, you need two things: the Poké Flute to wake up the annoying Snorlax who is blocking the road and a Bicycle. If you haven't already gone back to Cerulean City with your Bike Voucher, do so immediately. They don't call this area Cycling Road for nothing!

Wake the Snorlax

You won't get very far unless you wake this public nuisance and get him moving. If you haven't added one of these to your collection (there are only two of them), make sure that you nab this one. Just be patient and he'll eventually be yours.

Flight

Using the Cut ability, clear out the bush right before the Snorlax and head toward the northern gatehouse. On the other side is a house where a little girl will give you her HM 02 machine. This will allow any of your Flight Pokémon to transport you anywhere on the map—as long as you've been there before. This is a great way to travel to those out of the way places!

Trainer's Talk

Right outside the gate to Cycling Road you'll run into a gang of burly Bikers and Cue Balls. Their Pokémon, a combination of Poisonous and Normal/Fighting types, fluctuate between a puny LV 26 and a respectable LV 33. A piece of cake after some of the places you've been.

Route 17

Get ready to ride down an incredibly steep hill. It's so steep, in fact, that once you start, you'll have a hard time stopping until you reach the bottom!

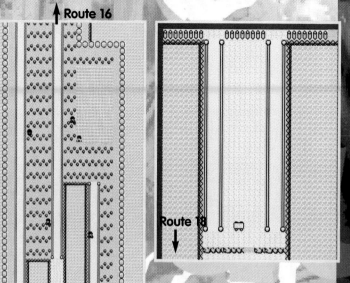

↑ Route 16

Route 18 ↓

Trainer's Talk

Unfortunately, you won't be able to ride fast enough to escape the Bikers and Cue Balls that have staked out spots on this road.

Route 16

Things to Get
1. HM 02 (Fly)

Any Pokémon?

	Red	Blue
Spearow	Common	Common
Rattata	Rare	Rare
Raticate	Rare	Rare
Doduo	Rare	Rare

Route 17

Things to Get

👁 None

Any Pokémon?

	Red	Blue
Spearow	Common	Common
Fearow	Rare	Rare
Rattata	Rare	Rare
Raticate	Rare	Rare
Doduo	Rare	Rare

👁 Fish for Tentacool, Krabby, Magikarp, and Goldeen.

Route 18

Route 18 lies at the bottom of Cycling Road. With the hill done and over, you can ride normally now. Fuchsia City is only a short distance away.

Trader Alert!

On the top floor of the gatehouse between Cycling Road and Fuchsia City is a person willing to trade his Lickitung for a lesser Slowbro. Get your Fishing Pole ready!

Things to Get

👁 None

Any Pokémon?

	Red	Blue
Spearow	Common	Common
Fearow	Rare	Rare
Rattata	Rare	Rare
Raticate	Rare	Rare
Doduo	Rare	Rare

👁 Fish for Tentacool, Krabby, Magikarp, and Goldeen.

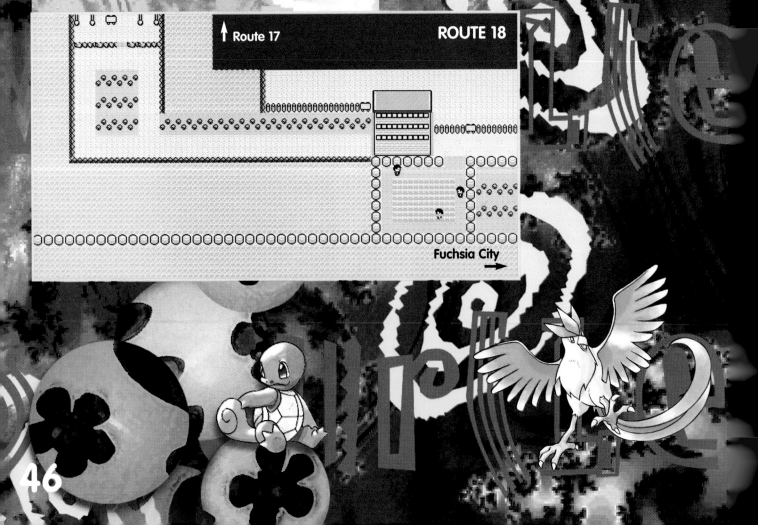

↑ Route 17   ROUTE 18

Fuchsia City →

Fuchsia City

At the southernmost part of the main Pokémon Continent lies the seaside town of Fuchsia. Here you'll find the famous Safari Zone, home to many rare and unique Pokémon.

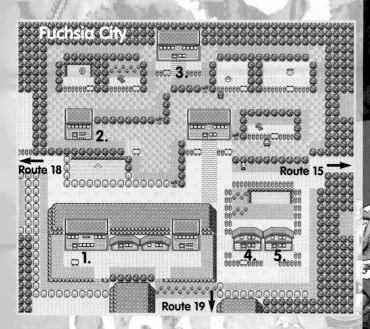

Fuchsia City

← Route 18

Route 15 →

↓ Route 19

1. Fuchsia Gym

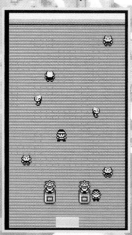

Gym Leader Koga has barricaded himself behind invisible walls just to make sure that you don't escape the hands of his Junior Trainers. However, if you're playing this on a Super Game Boy®, the walls just won't seem that invisible.

2. Shop near the Safari Zone

This shop is located next to the self-contained Safari Zone. You won't find any souvenirs here!

Merchandise

Ultra Ball	1,200P
Great Ball	600P
Super Potion	700P
Revive	1,500P
Full Heal	600P
Super Repel	500P

3. Safari Time

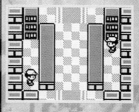

When you have few hours to spend, take on the Safari Zone. Here you'll find more Pokémon than you thought possible. Make sure that you have an empty box waiting for you on Bill's Computer, so that you don't have to make a journey back to the Pokémon Center.

4. Game Warden's House

The Game Warden would love to tell you all about his Strength, but he lost his false teeth while patrolling the grounds of the Safari Zone. Maybe if you help him out, he'd teach you how to move that heavy boulder.

5. Fishing Guru

This home belongs to the third Fishing Guru. If you haven't already picked up the Super Rod from his other brother on Route 12, then the Good Rod he gives you will seem fine until then.

Gym Leader Lowdown #6: Koga of the Fuchsia City Gym

The choice of Poisonous and Psychic Pokémon fulfills Koga's wish to fight by cleverness rather than strength. You've seen how many HP you can lose when poisoned or otherwise unable to fight, so he may have a point. However, if you've raised strong offensive fighters and are carrying a few Full Heals, you're going to walk all over his crafty monsters.

When you defeat him, Koga relinquishes his Soul Badge. This raises your Pokémon's defense and allows you to Surf the waves to the south, if and when you find HM 03. His present of TM 06 (Toxic) is also a helpful addition to your quest.

Koga's Pokémon Lineup

Koffing	LV 37
Muk	LV 39
Koffing	LV 37
Weezing	LV 43

Safari Zone

The Safari Zone is home to many rare and spectacular Pokémon. To catch them all will require some skill, but mostly luck. Prepare to spend a lot of time and money here if you plan to collect all 150 Pokémon.

Fuchsia City

Things to Do
◉ Defeat Koga at the Fuchsia City Gym.
◉ Get the Good Rod.
◉ Get HM 04 from the Game Warden.
◉ Visit the Safari Zone.

Places to Go
◉ Pokémon Center
◉ Poké Mart
◉ Fuchsia City Gym
◉ Safari Zone
◉ Game Warden's House
◉ Fishing Guru's House

Things to Get
◉ HM 04 (Strength)
◉ Good Rod
◉ Soul Badge
◉ TM 06 (Toxic)

Any Pokémon?
◉ Try fishing for Magikarp, Krabby, Goldeen, and Seaking.

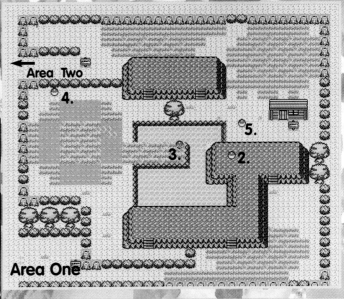

Area One

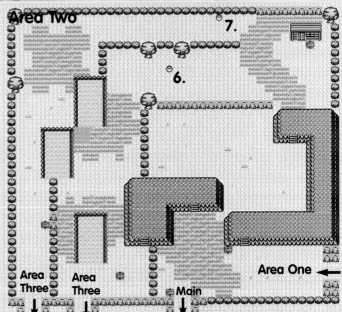

Area Two

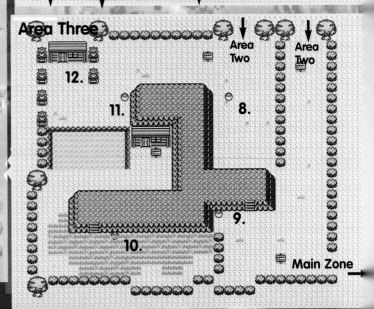

Area Three

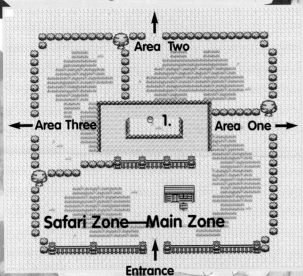

Safari Zone—Main Zone

The Way Things Work

You pay the 500P admission and in return you get 30 Safari Balls. These are specially made to catch the monsters in the Safari Zone. Don't expect it to be easy though. There are a lot of Pokémon that you can catch with one or two balls. The more rare and unique characters will need more coaxing. Rocks and Food may help, but the best way to catch them is by patiently tossing Safari Ball after Safari Ball at them.

Did I Mention the Time Limit?

You have roughly 500 seconds each time you're in the Safari Zone. In concrete terms you actually have 500 steps, since the timer starts whenever you stay still, fish, or get into a battle with a Pokémon. To check on your progress, merely bring up the Menu screen.

The Contest

If you can make it to the house in the northwest corner of Area 3 before your time runs out, you'll win a special prize: HM 03 (Surf). Not only will this help you Surf across the oceans to the islands in the south, but it'll help you get around the Safari Zone much quicker! In this same area, you'll also find the Game Warden's Gold Teeth.

Safari Zone

Things to Get

1. Nugget
2. Carbos
3. TM 37 (Egg Bomb)
4. Max Potion
5. Full Restore
6. TM 40 (Skull Bash)
7. Protein
8. Gold Teeth
9. Max Revive
10. Max Potion
11. TM 32 (Double Team)
12. HM 03 (Surf)

Any Pokémon?

Main Zone

		Red	Blue
♂	Nidoran	Rare	—
	Nidorino	Rare	Rare
♀	Nidoran	—	Rare
	Nidorina	Rare	Rare
	Rhyhorn	Rare	Rare
	Venonat	Rare	Rare
	Exeggcute	Rare	Rare
	Parasect	Rare	Rare
	Scyther	Rare	—
	Pinsir	—	Rare
	Chansey	Rare	Rare

Area I

		Red	Blue
♂	Nidoran	Rare	Rare
	Nidorino	Rare	—
♀	Nidoran	Rare	Rare
	Nidorina	—	Rare
	Doduo	Rare	Rare
	Exeggcute	Rare	Rare
	Paras	Rare	Rare
	Parasect	Rare	Rare
	Kangaskhan	Rare	Rare
	Scyther	Rare	—
	Pinsir	—	Rare

Area II

		Red	Blue
♂	Nidoran	Rare	—
	Nidorino	Rare	Rare
♀	Nidoran	—	Rare
	Nidorina	Rare	Rare
	Rhyhorn	Rare	Rare
	Exeggcute	Rare	Rare
	Paras	Rare	Rare
	Venomoth	Rare	Rare
	Tauros	Rare	Rare
	Chansey	Rare	Rare

Area III

	Red	Blue
♂ Nidoran	Rare	Rare
Nidorino	Rare	—
♀ Nidoran	Rare	Rare
Nidorina	—	Rare
Venonat	Rare	Rare
Venomoth	Rare	Rare
Doduo	Rare	Rare
Exeggcute	Rare	Rare
Tauros	Rare	Rare
Kangaskhan	Rare	Rare

Routes 19 and 20

Once you leave Fuchsia City, you'll be traveling by sea to the Seafoam Islands and the Gym on Cinnabar Island. This route is filled with wild Tentacool of varying experience levels from LV 5 to LV 30. If you need to pick one up for your collection, you'll get to pick whichever one you like.

Route 19

ROUTE 19

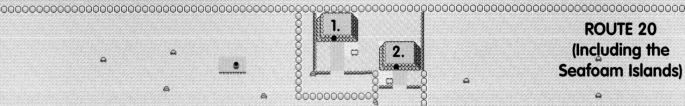

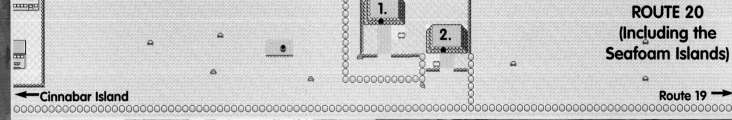

← Cinnabar Island

Route 19 →

ROUTE 20 (Including the Seafoam Islands)

Trainer's Talk

A group of Swimmers and Beauties rule this watery road. By this time, nothing they throw at you should come as a surprise. What will be surprising is the lack of money you'll make fighting these guys! Swimmers carry very little cash on them and unless you need the experience, they're not really worth fighting.

Twin Mountains

To enter the dungeon on the Seafoam Islands, you'll need to visit the left entrance first. The make your way through the cavern and come out on the other side. You have to exit through the door on the right mountain to continue on Route 20 to Cinnabar Island.

Routes 19 & 20

Things to Get
◉ None

Any Pokémon?

	Red	Blue
Tentacool	Common	Common

Seafoam Islands

In the middle of Route 20 lie the Seafoam Islands. This place is home to tons of Water Pokémon, many of whom you've probably only seen in Trainer Battles. The Seafoam Islands are also home to one of the legendary Pokémon, Articuno. This icy blue bird lies at the bottom of the cavern where the current is the strongest.

Seafoam Islands 1F

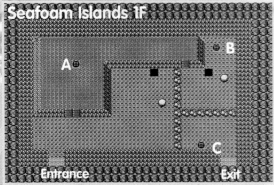

Seafoam Islands B1

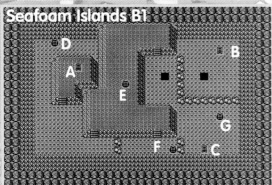

Seafoam Islands B2

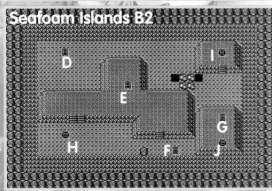

Seafoam Islands B3

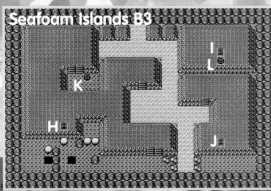

Seafoam Islands B4

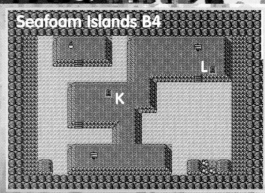

Use Your Strength

The last two floors of this dungeon are divided by a stream with an extremely fast current. So fast, that you won't be able to do much Surfing. To calm the current, you'll need to push the boulders you see lying around down the holes to the bottom floor. There are three boulders in the cave that will do the job. Can you figure this puzzle out?

Articuno

This bird is not easy to catch, but then the rarest species never are. First, before you storm into battle, save your game! This LV 50 bird is too precious to kill accidentally. Next, make sure you have about 50 or more Ultra Balls in your possession. Even paralyzed with a few HP left, Articuno is too vigorous to stay in an Ultra Ball and catching him will largely be a matter of luck and patience. Then, carefully whittle away at his HP. You don't want to use a Pokémon that is overly strong, but you'll want one who will last the battle. Start throwing Ultra Balls when you have Articuno down to a mere sliver of his HP gauge and … good luck.

Seafoam Islands

Things to Get

👁 None

Any Pokémon?

	Red	Blue
Zubat	Rare	Rare
Golbat	Rare	Rare
Seel	Rare	Rare
Dewgong	Rare	Rare
Slowpoke	Rare	Rare
Slowbro	Rare	Rare
Psyduck	Rare	Rare
Golduck	Rare	Rare
Shellder	Rare	Rare
Staryu	Rare	Rare
Horsea	Rare	—
Seadra	Rare	—
Krabby	—	Rare
Kingler	—	Rare

👁 Articuno

Cinnabar Island

Floating in the middle of the sea to the west of Seafoam Islands, lies tiny Cinnabar Island. There may not be much land here, but you'll still find yourself surrounded with action. Cinnabar has long been known as a place for Pokémon research. Head over to the Pokémon Lab and see what new research is being done. Or, if you have time, look at the abandoned research facilities in the Pokémon House. You might even learn about new species of Pokémon.

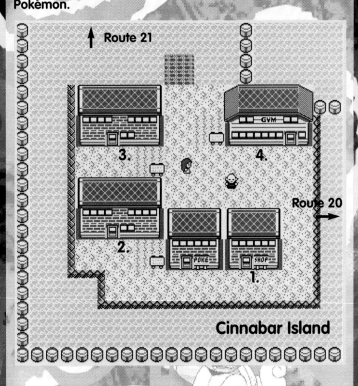

Cinnabar Island

2. The Pokémon Lab

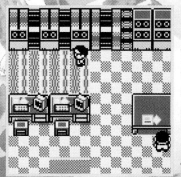

Inside the Lab, you'll find lots of people buzzing about Pokémon research. The room at the far end is even used to research fossils. Go get the fossils you got from Pewter City and Mt. Moon and let the Scientist look at them. I think he might actually be able to revive them.

Also, be on the lookout for traders. Some of them might even have something you're looking for.

3. Pokémon House

This once-ornate center of Pokémon learning has fallen into disuse and now Burglars roam about trying to find things to steal. They say that a certain key is found there ….

4. Cinnabar Island Gym

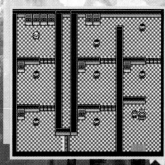

The door is locked. Find the key and battle your way through the hallways of Trainers to find the reclusive Blaine.

1. Poké Mart on the Sea

Here you'll find more outstanding wares at their usual prices.

Merchandise

Ultra Ball	1,200P
Great Ball	600P
Super Potion	1,500P
Max Repel	700P
Escape Rope	550P
Full Heal	600P
Revive	1,500P

Gym Leader Lowdown #7: Blaine at the Cinnabar Island Gym

Blaine tries as hard as he can to keep the public away. Not only has he locked the door with a well-hidden key, but then you have to fight Trainer after Trainer before you reach the final barricade! While you're doing that you'll have ample time to determine a strategy against Flame Pokémon. I'd suggest using a Water Pokémon or even a Ground/Rock type if you have one handy.

When he's been toasted, Blaine will give you his Volcano Badge. This increases your Pokémon's special skills! He'll also give you TM 38, which teaches a lucky Flame Pokémon the skill Fire Blast. That might come in handy against the Elite Four on Indigo Plateau.

Blaine's Pokémon Lineup

Growlithe	LV 42
Ponyta	LV 40
Rapidash	LV 42
Arcanine	LV 47

Cinnabar Island

Things to Do
- Resurrect your Fossils at the Pokémon Lab.
- Get the Secret Key from the Pokémon House.
- Defeat Blaine at the Cinnabar Island Gym.

Places to Go
- Pokémon Center
- Poké Mart
- Cinnabar Island Gym
- Pokémon Lab
- Pokémon House

Things to Get
- Secret Key
- Volcano Badge
- TM 35 (Metronome)
- TM 38 (Fire Blast)

Any Pokémon?
- Try fishing for Staryu, Horsea, Shellder, and Goldeen.

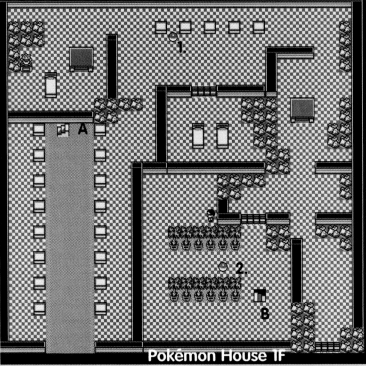

Pokémon House 1F

Pokémon House

This abandoned and rotting house is now only home to a bunch of Poisonous and Fire Pokémon and Burglars. There's supposed to be a Secret Key somewhere around here.

Pokémon House 2F

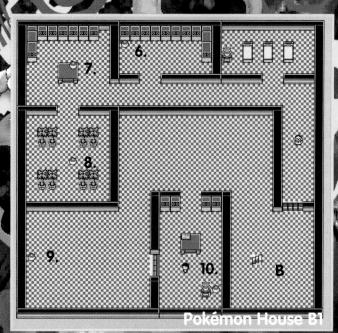

Pokémon House B1

Pokémon House 3F

Pokémon House

Things to Get
1. Escape Rope
2. Carbos
3. Calcium
4. Max Potion
5. Iron
6. Rare Candy
7. TM 22 (Solarbeam)
8. Secret Key
9. Full Restore
10. TM 14 (Blizzard)

Any Pokémon?

	Red	Blue
Koffing	Common	Rare
Weezing	Rare	Rare
Grimer	Rare	Common
Ponyta	Common	Common
Growlithe	Rare	—
Vulpix	—	Rare
Magmar	—	Rare

Trainer's Talk
The Scientists and Burglars in this house will serve as a good warm up for Blaine and the Trainers at the Cinnabar Island Gym. If you can beat these Trainers easily, you'll do fine against Blaine.

Hidden Switches
There are switches hidden in the statues. If you pull one, certain doors will open and others will close. One pull of the switch effects the whole house. Remember this if you think you're stuck.

No Stairs to the Basement
Well, of course, the key is in the basement. But how are you going to get there? The only way down seems to be by jumping…from the third floor, of course! Try the open area to the left of the Scientist. That seems to be the fastest way down.

Route 21

Finally, once you surf down this path, you'll have come full circle. The waterway will take you straight to Pallet Town, where you're only a short journey away from Viridian City and the eighth Badge.

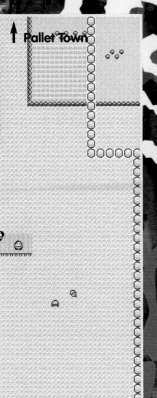

↑ Pallet Town

ROUTE 21

Cinnabar Island ↓

Things to Get
1. Escape Rope
2. Carbos
3. Calcium
4. Max Potion
5. Iron
6. Rare Candy
7. TM 22 (Solarbeam)
8. Secret Key
9. Full Restore
10. TM 14 (Blizzard)

Any Pokémon?

	Red	Blue
Koffing	Common	Rare
Weezing	Rare	Rare
Grimer	Rare	Common
Ponyta	Common	Common
Growlithe	Rare	—
Vulpix	—	Rare
Magmar	—	Rare

More Trainer's Talk?

If you're tired of fighting, hug the wall to the left and you'll stay out of the path of all of the Trainers on this route. They're the usual lot of Swimmers with a few Fishermen standing on piers in the middle of the water. Fight them if you think that your Pokémon need the practice and the added experience, but if you're dying to get to the end, it's OK if you skip them.

Route 21

Things to Get
👁 None

Any Pokémon?

	Red	Blue
Rattata	Rare	Rare
Raticate	Rare	Rare
Pidgey	Rare	Rare
Pigeotto	Rare	Rare
Tangela	Rare	Rare
Tentacool	Common	Common

Should I Make a Pitstop?

The plot of grass south of Pallet Town is home to the usual Pokémon, except for one. In these thickets, and these thickets alone, you'll find the rare Tangela. So, stopping here to hunt is a good idea.

Route 22

Hopefully this street isn't new to you or you missed out on a good opportunity to catch some Nidoran early on in the game. At the end of the road lies the entrance to Route 23 and Victory Road. Before you can walk through the doors, you'll have to have all eight Badges in your possession. Guards posted along Route 23 will check, so don't try to fool them.

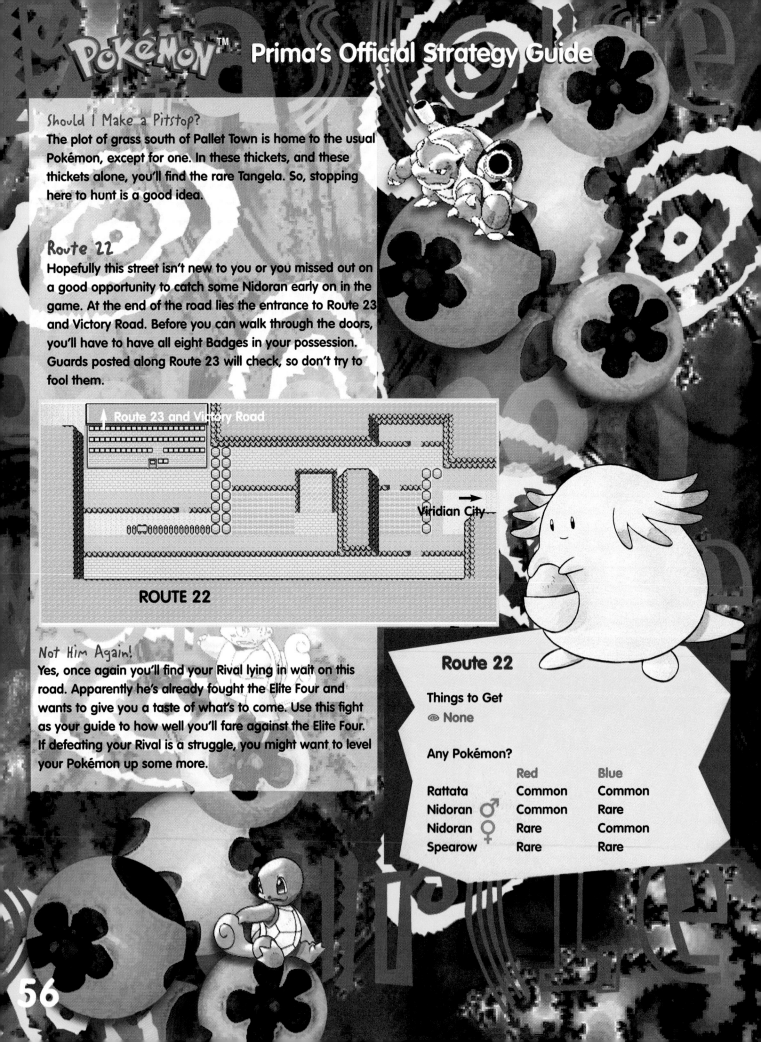

↑ Route 23 and Victory Road

Viridian City →

ROUTE 22

Not Him Again!

Yes, once again you'll find your Rival lying in wait on this road. Apparently he's already fought the Elite Four and wants to give you a taste of what's to come. Use this fight as your guide to how well you'll fare against the Elite Four. If defeating your Rival is a struggle, you might want to level your Pokémon up some more.

Route 22

Things to Get
◉ None

Any Pokémon?

	Red	Blue
Rattata	Common	Common
Nidoran ♂	Common	Rare
Nidoran ♀	Rare	Common
Spearow	Rare	Rare

Route 23

You finally made it. At the end of this long road lies the entrance to Victory Road and the Indigo Plateau. You won't find any Trainers here to spoil things but there are lots of uncommon Pokémon wandering around. Check your list and see if you need anything to complete your collection before you go up against the Elite Four.

Route 23

Things to Get

👁 None

Any Pokémon?

	Red	Blue
Ditto	Rare	Rare
Spearow	Rare	Rare
Fearow	Rare	Rare
Ekans	Rare	—
Arbok	Rare	—
Sandshrew	—	Rare
Sandslash	—	Rare

👁 Fish for Slowbro, Kingler, Seadra, and Seaking.

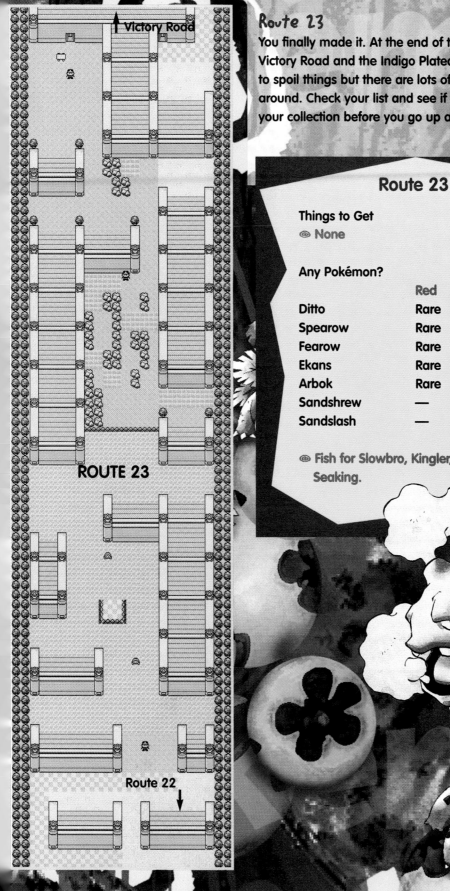

↑ Victory Road

ROUTE 23

Route 22 ↓

Victory Road 1F

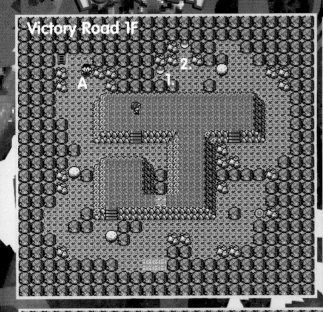

Victory Road 2F

Victory Road 3F

Victory Road

The dungeon known as Victory Road is the final proving ground for young Trainers wanting to go up against the Elite Four. You will face tough challenges here from the Trainers and the puzzles. Before you leave and enter Indigo Plateau, you will want to try to catch another legendary bird, Moltos.

Boulder + Pressure Plate = ?

The pressure plates hold the stone doors open, but you can't be in two places at once. Try pushing the boulders over to the pressure plates to hold them open.

Two Routes

There are two routes that you can take in Victory Road. Using stairs A, B, and C will take you to the exit while detouring to stairs D and E will take you to Moltos' lair.

Moltos

This legendary Flame Bird is just as hard to catch as Articuno in the Seafoam Islands. Use the same techniques to weaken and capture it as you did with Articuno and you should be fine. Remember to save before you approach him though!

Victory Road

Things to Get

1. Rare Candy
2. TM 43 (Sky Attack)
3. TM 05 (Mega Kick)
4. Full Heal
5. TM 17 (Submission)
6. Guard Spec.
7. Max Revive
8. Full Restore

Any Pokémon?

	Red	Blue
Machop	Rare	Rare
Machoke	Rare	Rare
Geodude	Rare	Rare
Graveler	Rare	Rare
Zubat	Rare	Rare
Golbat	Rare	Rare
Onix	Rare	Rare
Marowak	Rare	Rare
Venomoth	Rare	Rare

Indigo Plateau

Finally—the end. I hope you weren't expecting a full-fledged city or something? Indigo Plateau combines the best of a Poké Mart with all the conveniences of a Pokémon Center. You can heal your Pokémon and buy the most powerful Potions here before your big encounter with the Elite Four.

Tons of New Merchandise at Cutthroat Prices!

Ultra Ball	1,200P
Great Ball	600P
Full Restore	3,000P
Max Potion	2,500P
Full Heal	600P
Revive	1,500
Max Repel	700P

Lorelei: Master Trainer of Water Pokémon

Lorelei is probably the easiest of the Elite Four, but that's not saying much. Use Electric or Grass Pokémon and you'll be fine. It's a good thing that you've had so much practice against them.

Lorelei's Lineup

Dewgong	LV 54
Cloyster	LV 53
Slowbro	LV 54
Jynx	LV 56
Lapras	LV 56

Bruno: Master Trainer of Ground and Fighting Pokémon

These hard-core fighters aren't nearly as intimidating as they think. Attack them with Water, Flight, or Psychic skills and they're toast.

Bruno's Lineup

Onix	LV 53
Hitmonchan	LV 55
Hitmonlee	LV 55
Onix	LV 56
Machamp	LV 58

Agatha: Master Trainer of Ghost and Poison Pokémon

As you learned in the Pokémon Tower, fighting Ghost Pokémon is no fun at all. Agatha's have a severe tendency to cast Confuse Ray and Nightshade which will make your Pokémon feel pretty loopy. Counter the best you can, using the same techniques you developed in the Pokémon Tower.

Agatha's Lineup

Gengar	LV 56
Golbat	LV 56
Haunter	LV 55
Arbok	LV 58
Gengar	LV 60

Lance: Master Trainer of Dragon Pokémon

Dragons are something rarely seen in the world of Pokémon, so don't be surprised if you don't quite know how to handle them. An Ice Pokémon seems to be very effective against them, as does another Dragon. Any final-form Pokémon outfitted with the skill Hyper Beam (purchased at the Coin Exchange in Celadon City) should be able to take these Pokémon out with one stroke.

Lance's Lineup

Gyrados	LV 58
Dragonair	LV 56
Dragonair	LV 56
Aerodactyl	LV 60
Dragonite	LV 62

Final Battle Against Your Rival

The Pokémon your Rival chose at the beginning of the game determines the lineup he'll have here at the end. Your Rival has compiled a very well-rounded band of Pokémon to fight against you. He has representatives of all of the major groups (Psychic, Flight, Ground, Water, Fire, and Grass), and you'll want to have a troop of Pokémon that can counter them. This is probably the toughest fight you'll have in the game, so remember all that you've learned and good luck!

Rival's Lineup

Pidgeot	LV 61
Alakazam	LV 59
Rhydon	LV 61

Pattern One	Pattern Two	Pattern Three
Arcanine LV 61	Gyarados LV 61	Exeggutor LV 63
Exeggutor LV 63	Arcanine LV 63	Gyarados LV 61
Blastoise LV 65	Venusaur LV 65	Charizard LV 65

Aftermath

So the game ends. But does it really? You still have lots of Pokémon to collect and you haven't even explored the Unknown Dungeon. Take heart. Once you finish this battle, your game is saved and restarts back at the Pallet Town Pokémon Center. From there you can roam the world freely collecting as many Pokémon as you want. You can even take on the Elite Four as many times as you like (it's a great way to level up your Pokémon).

Power Plant

You can access the Power Plant once you've learned the Surf ability. Inside you'll find a ton of Electric Pokémon and the third of the Bird Trio, the legendary Zapdos.

Power Plant

Item Ball or Voltorb?

It's hard to tell the difference, isn't it? You can only really tell when you pick one up. If it comes alive, then you guessed wrong.

Zapdos

Right before the exit of the Power Plant you'll find the Electric Bird Zapdos. If you're a fan of Electric Pokémon then you definitely want to add this bird to your arsenal. Save before approaching and capture him using the same techniques as you used with his brethren.

Indigo Plateau

Things to Get
1. Carbos
2. TM 33 (Reflect)
3. TM 25 (Thunder)
4. Rare Candy
5. HP Up

Any Pokémon?

	Red	Blue
Voltorb	Rare	Rare
Magnemite	Rare	Rare
Magneton	Rare	Rare
Pikachu	Rare	Rare
Raichu	—	Rare
Electabuzz	Rare	—

Unknown Dungeon

The final dungeon only becomes accessible after you've completed a bout against the Elite Four and finished the game. Then the sentry blocking your way leaves and the Unknown Dungeon becomes your play-ground.

There are lots of rare Pokémon here running around wild, so stock up on Ultra Balls and happy hunting.

Warning: High-Level Monsters Inside!

Unknown Dungeon is known for the pow-erful and dangerous monsters inside. They range in experience from LV 50 on up. The Mewtwo that you can capture in the base-ment is a tough LV 70.

Unknown Dungeon 1F

ENTRANCE

Unknown Dungeon 2F

Unknown Dungeon B1

Mewtwo

You read about him in the Pokémon House on Cinnabar Island and now he's staring you in the face. It's possible to capture him in the same way as the Bird Trio, but you might just want to skip the hassle and use your Master Ball instead.

Unknown Dungeon

Things to Get

1. Max Ether	5. PP Up
2. Nugget	6. Ultra Ball
3. Full Restore	7. Max Revive
4. Full Restore	8. Ultra Ball

Any Pokémon?

	Red	Blue
Golbat	Rare	Rare
Hypno	Rare	Rare
Magneton	Rare	Rare
Dodrio	Rare	Rare
Venomoth	Rare	Rare
Kadabra	Rare	Rare
Parasect	Rare	Rare
Raichu	Rare	Rare
Ditto	Rare	Rare
Rhydon	Rare	Rare
Marowak	Rare	Rare
Electrode	Rare	Rare
Chansey	Rare	Rare
Wigglytuff	Rare	Rare
Arbok	Rare	—
Sandslash	—	Rare

The Complete Pokédex

This appendix gives you the most information possible about each of the 150 creatures inhabiting Pokémon Island. If you want to know when a certain monster evolves or how long until it learns that next skill, then look no further! The complete Pokédex also tells you where to find each monster and what skills you can teach them—besides the ones they already know.

Bulbasaur—No. 01

Evolution: No. 02. Ivysaur (LV 16), No. 03. Venusaur (LV 32)

Vital Statistics
Type: Grass/Poison
Height: 2'4" Weight: 15 lbs
Appearance: Prof. Oak's Lab (Pallet Town)
Description: A strange seed was planted on its back at birth, which sprouts and grows with this Pokémon.

Learned Skill List:

Level	Skill	Type
—	Tackle	Normal
—	Growl	Normal
LV 7	Leech Seed	Grass
LV 13	Vine Whip	Grass
LV 20	Poison Powder	Poison
LV 27	Razor Leaf	Grass
LV 34	Growth	Normal
LV 41	Sleep Powder	Grass
LV 48	Solarbeam	Grass

Technical Machines: 03, 06, 08, 09, 10, 20, 21, 22, 31, 32, 33, 34, 44, 50
Hidden Machines: 01

Ivysaur—No. 02

Evolution: No. 03. Venusaur (LV 32)

Vital Statistics
Type: Grass/Poison
Height: 3'3" Weight: 29 lbs
Appearance: —
Description: As the bulb on its back grows larger, it appears to lose the ability to stand on its hind legs.

Learned Skill List:

Level	Skill	Type
—	Tackle	Normal
—	Growl	Normal
—	Leech Seed	Grass
—	Vine Whip	Grass
LV 22	Poison Powder	Poison
LV 30	Razor Leaf	Grass
LV 38	Growth	Normal
LV 46	Sleep Powder	Grass
LV 54	Solarbeam	Grass

Technical Machines: 03, 06, 08, 09, 10, 20, 21, 22, 31, 32, 33, 34, 44, 50
Hidden Machines: 01

Venusaur—No. 03

Evolution: Final Stage

Vital Statistics
Type: Grass/Poison
Height: 6'7" Weight: 221 lbs
Appearance: —
Description: The plant blooms when it is absorbing solar energy, prompting the Venusaur to keep moving in search of sunlight.

Learned Skill List:

Level	Skill	Type
—	Tackle	Normal
—	Growl	Normal
—	Leech Seed	Grass
—	Vine Whip	Grass
—	Poison Powder	Poison
—	Razor Leaf	Grass
LV 43	Growth	Normal
LV 55	Sleep Powder	Grass
LV 65	Solarbeam	Grass

Technical Machines: 03, 06, 08, 09, 10, 15, 20, 21, 22, 31, 32, 33, 34, 44, 50
Hidden Machines: 01

Charmander—No. 04

Evolution: No. 05. Charmeleon (LV 16), No. 06. Charizard (LV 36)

Vital Statistics
Type: Fire
Height: 2'0" Weight: 19 lbs
Appearance: Prof. Oak's Lab (Pallet Town)
Description: Obviously prefers hot places. When it rains, steam is said to spout from the tip of its tail.

Learned Skill List:

Level	Skill	Type
—	Scratch	Normal
—	Growl	Normal
LV 9	Ember	Fire
LV 15	Leer	Normal
LV 22	Rage	Normal
LV 30	Slash	Normal
LV 38	Flamethrower	Fire
LV 46	Fire Spin	Fire

Technical Machines: 01, 03, 05, 06, 08, 09, 10, 17, 18, 19, 20, 23, 28, 31, 32, 33, 34, 38, 39, 40, 44, 50
Hidden Machines: 01, 04

Charmeleon—05

Evolution: No. 06. Charizard (LV 36)

Vital Statistics
Type: Fire
Height: 3'7" Weight: 42 lbs
Appearance: —
Description: When it swings its burning tail, it elevates the temperature around it to unbearably high levels.

Learned Skill List:

Level	Skill	Type
—	Scratch	Normal
—	Growl	Normal
—	Ember	Fire
—	Leer	Normal
LV 24	Rage	Normal
LV 33	Slash	Normal
LV 42	Flamethrower	Fire
LV 56	Fire Spin	Fire

Technical Machines: 01, 03, 05, 06, 08, 09, 10, 17, 18, 19, 20, 23, 28, 31, 32, 33, 34, 38, 39, 40, 44, 50
Hidden Machines: 01, 04

Charizard—No. 06

Evolution: Final Stage

Vital Statistics
Type: Fire/Flying
Height: 5'7" Weight: 200 lbs
Appearance: —
Description: Spits fire that is hot enough to melt boulders. Known to cause forest fires unintentionally.

Learned Skill List:

Level	Skill	Type
—	Scratch	Normal
—	Growl	Normal
—	Ember	Fire
—	Leer	Normal
—	Rage	Normal
LV 36	Slash	Normal
LV 46	Flamethrower	Fire
LV 55	Fire Spin	Fire

Technical Machines: 01, 03, 05, 06, 08, 09, 10, 17, 18, 19, 20, 23, 28, 31, 32, 33, 34, 38, 39, 40, 44, 50
Hidden Machines: 01, 04

Squirtle—No. 07

Evolution: No. 08. Wartortle (LV 16), No. 09. Blastoise (LV 36)

Vital Statistics
Type: Water
Height: 1'8" Weight: 20 lbs
Appearance: Prof. Oak's Lab (Pallet Town)
Description: After birth, its back swells and hardens into a shell. Powerfully sprays foam from its mouth.

Learned Skill List:

Level	Skill	Type
—	Tackle	Normal
—	Tail Whip	Normal
LV 8	Bubble	Water
LV 15	Water Gun	Water Gun
LV 22	Bite	Normal
LV 28	Withdraw	Water
LV 35	Skull Bash	Normal
LV 42	Hydro Pump	Water

Technical Machines: 01, 05, 06, 08, 09, 10, 11, 12, 13, 14, 17, 18, 19, 20, 28, 31, 32, 33, 34, 40, 44, 50
Hidden Machines: 03, 04

Wartortle—No. 08

Evolution: No. 09. Blastoise (LV 36)

Vital Statistics
Type: Water
Height: 3'3" Weight: 50 lbs
Appearance: —
Description: Often hides in water to stalk unwary prey. When swimming fast, it moves its ears to maintain its balance.

Learned Skill List:
Level	Skill	Type
—	Tackle	Normal
—	Tail Whip	Normal
—	Bubble	Water
LV 15	Water Gun	Water Gun
LV 24	Bite	Normal
LV 31	Withdraw	Water
LV 39	Skull Bash	Normal
LV 47	Hydro Pump	Water

Technical Machines: 01, 05, 06, 08, 09, 10, 11, 12, 13, 14, 17, 18, 19, 20, 28, 31, 32, 33, 34, 40, 44, 50
Hidden Machines: 03, 04

Blastoise—No. 09

Evolution: Final Stage

Vital Statistics
Type: Water
Height: 5'3" Weight: 189 lbs
Appearance: —
Description: A brutal Pokémon who has pressurized water jets on its shell used for high-speed tackles.

Learned Skill List
Level	Skill	Type
—	Tackle	Normal
—	Tail Whip	Normal
—	Bubble	Water
—	Water Gun	Water Gun
LV 24	Bite	Normal
LV 31	Withdraw	Water
LV 42	Skull Bash	Normal
LV 52	Hydro Pump	Water

Technical Machines: 01, 05, 06, 08, 09, 10, 11, 12, 13, 14, 15, 17, 18, 19, 20, 26, 27, 28, 31, 32, 33, 34, 40, 44, 50
Hidden Machines: 03, 04

Caterpie—No. 10

Evolution: No. 11. Metapod (LV 7), No. 12. Butterfree (LV 10)

Vital Statistics
Type: Bug
Height: 1'0" Weight: 6 lbs
Appearance: Viridian Forest; Routes 2, 24, and 25
Description: Its short feet are tipped with suction pads that enable it to tirelessly climb slopes and walls.

Learned Skill List:
Level	Skill	Type
—	Tackle	Normal
—	String Shot	Bug

Technical Machines: N/A
Hidden Machines: N/A

Metapod—No. 11

Evolution: No. 12. Butterfree (LV 10)

Vital Statistics
Type: Bug
Height: 2'4" Weight: 22 lbs
Appearance: Viridian Forest; Routes 2, 24, and 25
Description: This Pokémon is vulnerable to attack while its shell is soft, exposing its weak and tender body.

Learned Skill List:
Level	Skill	Type
—	Harden	Normal

Technical Machines: N/A
Hidden Machines: N/A

Butterfree—No. 12

Evolution: Final Form

Vital Statistics
Type: Bug/Flying
Height: 3'7" Weight: 71 lbs
Appearance: —
Description: In battle, it flaps its wings at high speed, releasing highly toxic dust into the air.

Learned Skill List:
Level	Skill	Type
LV 12	Confusion	Psychic
LV 15	Poison Powder	Poison
LV 16	Stun Spore	Grass
LV 17	Sleep Powder	Grass
LV 21	Supersonic	Normal
LV 26	Whirlwind	Normal
LV 32	Psybeam	Psychic

Technical Machines: 02, 04, 06, 09, 10, 15, 20, 21, 22, 29, 30, 31, 32, 33, 34, 39, 44, 46, 50
Hidden Machines: N/A

Weedle—No. 13

Evolution: No. 14. Kakuna (LV 7), No. 15 Beedrill (LV 10)

Vital Statistics
Type: Bug/Poison
Height: 1'0" Weight: 7 lbs
Appearance: Viridian Forest; Routes 2, 24, and 25
Description: Often found in forests, eating leaves. It has a sharp, venomous stinger on its head.

Learned Skill List:
Level	Skill	Type
—	Poison Sting	Poison
—	String Shot	Bug

Technical Machines: N/A
Hidden Machines: N/A

Kakuna—No. 14

Evolution: No. 15. Beedril (LV 10)

Vital Statistics
Type: Bug/Poison
Height: 2'0" Weight: 22 lbs
Appearance: Viridian Forest; Routes 2, 24, and 25
Description: Almost incapable of moving, this Pokémon can only harden its shell to protect itself from predators.

Learned Skill List:
Level	Skill	Type
—	Harden	Normal

Technical Machines: N/A
Hidden Machines: N/A

Beedrill—No. 15

Evolution: Final Form

Vital Statistics
Type: Bug/Poison
Height: 3'3" Weight: 65 lbs
Appearance: —
Description: Flies at high speeds and attacks using the large venomous stingers on its forelegs and tails.

Learned Skill List:
Level	Skill	Type
LV 12	Fury Attack	Normal
LV 16	Focus Energy	Normal
LV 20	Twineedle	Bug
LV 25	Rage	Normal
LV 30	Pin Missile	Bug
LV 35	High Speed	Psychic

Technical Machines: 03, 06, 09, 10, 15, 20, 21, 31, 32, 33, 34, 39, 40, 44, 50
Hidden Machines: 01

Pidgey—No. 16

Evolution: No. 17. Pidgeotto (LV 18), No. 18. Pidgeot (LV 36)

Vital Statistics
Type: Normal/Flying
Height: 1'0" Weight: 4 lbs
Appearance: Routes 1, 2, 3, 5, 6, 7, 8, 12, 14, 15, 24, and 25
Description: A common sight in the forests and woods, it flaps its wings at ground level to kick up blinding sand.

Learned Skill List:
Level	Skill	Type
—	Gust	Flying
LV 5	Sand Attack	Normal
LV 12	Quick Attack	Normal
LV 19	Whirlwind	Normal
LV 28	Wing Attack	Flying
LV 36	Agility	Psychic
LV 44	Mirror Move	Flying

Technical Machines: 02, 03, 06, 09, 10, 20, 31, 32, 33, 34, 39, 43, 44, 50
Hidden Machines: 02

Pidgeotto—No. 17

Evolution: **No. 18. Pidgeot (LV 36)**

Vital Statistics
Type: **Normal/Flying**
Height: **3'7"** Weight: **66 lbs**
Appearance: **Routes 14, 15, and 21**
Description: **Very protective of its sprawling territory, this Pokémon will fiercely peck at any intruder.**

Learned Skill List:

Level	Skill	Type
—	Gust	Flying
—	Sand Attack	Normal
—	Quick Attack	Normal
LV 21	Whirlwind	Normal
LV 31	Wing Attack	Flying
LV 40	Agility	Psychic
LV 49	Mirror Move	Flying

Technical Machines: 02, 03, 06, 09, 10, 20, 31, 32, 33, 34, 39, 43, 44, 50
Hidden Machines: 02

Pidgeot—No. 18

Evolution: **Final Form**

Vital Statistics
Type: **Normal/Flying**
Height: **4'11"** Weight: **87 lbs**
Appearance: —
Description: **When hunting, it skims the surface of water at high speed to pick off unwary prey, like Magikarp.**

Learned Skill List:

Level	Skill	Type
—	Gust	Flying
—	Sand Attack	Normal
—	Quick Attack	Normal
—	Whirlwind	Normal
—	Wing Attack	Flying
LV 44	Agility	Psychic
LV 54	Mirror Move	Flying

Technical Machines: 02, 03, 06, 09, 10, 15, 20, 31, 32, 33, 34, 39, 43, 44, 50
Hidden Machines: 02

Rattata—No. 19

Evolution: **No. 20. Raticate (LV 20)**

Vital Statistics
Type: **Normal**
Height: **1'0"** Weight: **8 lbs**
Appearance: **Routes 1, 2, 4, 9, 10, 16, 17, 18, 21, and 22**
Description: **Bites anything when it attacks. Small and very quick, it is a common sight in many places.**

Learned Skill List:

Level	Skill	Type
—	Tackle	Normal
—	Tail Whip	Normal
LV 7	Quick Attack	Normal
LV 14	Hyper Fang	Normal
LV 23	Focus Energy	Normal
LV 34	Super Fang	Normal

Technical Machines: 06, 08, 09, 10, 11, 12, 14, 20, 24, 25, 28, 31, 32, 34, 39, 40, 44, 50
Hidden Machines: N/A

Raticate—No. 20

Evolution: **Final Form**

Vital Statistics
Type: **Normal**
Height: **2'4"** Weight: **41 lbs**
Appearance: **Routes 16, 17, 18, and 21**
Description: **It uses its whiskers to maintain its balance and will slow down if they are cut off.**

Learned Skill List:

Level	Skill	Type
—	Tackle	Normal
—	Tail Whip	Normal
—	Quick Attack	Normal
LV 14	Hyper Fang	Normal
LV 27	Focus Energy	Normal
LV 41	Super Fang	Normal

Technical Machines: 06, 08, 09, 10, 11, 12, 13, 14, 15, 20, 24, 25, 28, 31, 32, 34, 39, 40, 44, 50
Hidden Machines: N/A

Spearow—No. 21

Evolution: **No. 22. Fearow (LV 20)**

Vital Statistics
Type: **Normal/Flying**
Height: **1'0"** Weight: **4 lbs**
Appearance: **Routes 3, 4, 9, 10, 11, 16, 17, 18, 22, and 23**
Description: **Eats bugs in grassy areas. Spearow has to flap its short wings at high speed to stay airborne.**

Learned Skill List:

Level	Skill	Type
—	Peck	Flying
—	Growl	Normal
LV 9	Leer	Normal
LV 15	Fury Attack	Normal
LV 22	Mirror Move	Flying
LV 29	Drill Peck	Flying
LV 36	Agility	Psychic

Technical Machines: 02, 04, 06, 09, 10, 20, 31, 32, 34, 39, 43, 44, 50
Hidden Machines: 02

Fearow—No. 22

Evolution: **Final Stage**

Vital Statistics
Type: **Normal/Flying**
Height: **3'11"** Weight: **84 lbs**
Appearance: **Routes 17, 18, and 23**
Description: **With its huge and magnificent wings, it can stay aloft without ever having to land for rest.**

Learned Skill List:

Level	Skill	Type
—	Peck	Flying
—	Growl	Normal
—	Leer	Normal
LV 15	Fury Attack	Normal
LV 25	Mirror Move	Flying
LV 34	Drill Peck	Flying
LV 43	Agility	Psychic

Technical Machines: 02, 04, 06, 09, 10, 15, 20, 31, 32, 34, 39, 43, 44, 50
Hidden Machines: 02

Ekans—No. 23

Evolution: **No. 24 Arbok (LV 22)**

Vital Statistics
Type: **Poison**
Height: **6' 7"** Weight: **15 lbs**
Appearance: **Routes 4, 8, 9, 10, 11, and 23**
Description: **Moves silently and stealthily and eats the eggs of birds such as Pidgey and Spearow whole.**

Learned Skill List:

Level	Skill	Type
—	Wrap	Normal
—	Leer	Normal
LV 10	Poison Sting	Poison
LV 17	Bite	Normal
LV 24	Glare	Normal
LV 31	Screech	Normal
LV 38	Acid	Poison

Technical Machines: 06, 08, 09, 10, 20, 21, 26, 27, 28, 31, 32, 34, 40, 44, 48, 50
Hidden Machines: 04

Arbok—No. 24

Evolution: **Final Stage**

Vital Statistics
Type: **Poison**
Height: **11' 6"** Weight: **143 lbs**
Appearance: **Route 23 and Unknown Dungeon**
Description: **It's rumored that the ferocious warning markings on its belly differ from area to area.**

Learned Skill List:

Level	Skill	Type
—	Wrap	Normal
—	Leer	Normal
—	Poison Sting	Poison
LV 17	Bite	Normal
LV 27	Glare	Normal
LV 36	Screech	Normal
LV 47	Acid	Poison

Technical Machines: 06, 08, 09, 10, 15, 20, 21, 26, 27, 28, 31, 32, 34, 40, 44, 48, 50
Hidden Machines: 04

Pikachu—No. 25

Evolution: **No. 26 Raichu (Thunder Stone)**

Vital Statistics
Type: **Electric**
Height: **1'4"** Weight: **13 lbs**
Appearance: **Viridian Forest and Power Plant**
Description: **When several of these Pokémon gather, their electricity could build and cause lightning storms.**

Learned Skill List:

Level	Skill	Type
—	Thundershock	Electric
—	Growl	Normal
LV 9	Thunderwave	Electric
LV 16	Quick Attack	Normal
LV 26	Swift	Normal
LV 33	Agility	Psychic
LV 43	Thunder	Electric

Technical Machines: 01, 05, 06, 08, 09, 10, 16, 17, 19, 20, 24, 25, 31, 32, 33, 34, 39, 40, 44, 45, 50
Hidden Machines: 05

Raichu—No. 26

Evolution: Final Form

Vital Statistics
Type: Electric
Height: 2'7" Weight: 66 lbs
Appearance: Power Plant and Unknown Dungeon
Description: Its long tail serves as a ground to protect itself from its own high voltage power.

Learned Skill List:

Level	Skill	Type
—	Thundershock	Electric
—	Growl	Normal
—	Thunderwave	Electric

Technical Machines: 01, 05, 06, 08, 09, 10, 15, 16, 17, 19, 20, 24, 25, 31, 32, 33, 34, 39, 40, 44, 45, 50
Hidden Machines: 05

Sandshrew—No. 27

Evolution: No. 28 Sandslash (LV 22)

Vital Statistics
Type: Ground
Height: 2'0" Weight: 26 lbs
Appearance: Routes 4, 8, 9, 10, 11, and 23
Description: Burrows deep underground in arid locations far from water and only emerges to hunt for food.

Learned Skill List:

Level	Skill	Type
—	Scratch	Normal
LV 10	Sand Attack	Normal
LV 17	Slash	Normal
LV 24	Poison Sting	Poison
LV 31	Swift	Normal
LV 38	Fury Swipes	Normal

Technical Machines: 03, 06, 08, 09, 10, 17, 19, 20, 26, 27, 28, 31, 32, 34, 39, 40, 44, 48, 50
Hidden Machines: 01, 04

Sandslash—No. 28

Evolution: Final Form

Vital Statistics
Type: Ground
Height: 3'3" Weight: 65 lbs
Appearance: Route 23 and Unknown Dungeon
Description: Curls up into a spiny ball when threatened. It can roll while curled up to hunt for food.

Learned Skill List:

Level	Skill	Type
—	Scratch	Normal
—	Sand Attack	Normal
—	Slash	Normal
LV 27	Poison Sting	Poison
LV 36	Swift	Normal
LV 47	Fury Swipes	Normal

Technical Machines: 03, 06, 08, 09, 10, 15, 17, 19, 20, 26, 27, 28, 31, 32, 34, 39, 40, 44, 48, 50
Hidden Machines: 01, 04

Nidoran ♀—No. 29

Evolution: No. 30 Nidorina (LV 16), Nidoqueen (Moon Stone)

Vital Statistics
Type: Poison
Height: 1'4" Weight: 15 lbs
Appearance: Route 22 and the Safari Zone
Description: Although small, its venomous barbs render this Pokémon dangerous. The female has smaller horns.

Learned Skill List:

Level	Skill	Type
—	Growl	Normal
—	Tackle	Normal
LV 8	Scratch	Normal
LV 14	Poison Sting	Poison
LV 21	Tail Whip	Normal
LV 29	Bite	Normal
LV 36	Fury Swipes	Normal
LV 43	Double Kick	Fighting

Technical Machines: 06, 08, 09, 10, 14, 20, 24, 25, 31, 32, 33, 34, 40, 44, 50
Hidden Machines: N/A

Nidorina—No. 30

Evolution: Nidoqueen (Moon Stone)

Vital Statistics
Type: Poison
Height: 2'7" Weight: 44 lbs
Appearance: Safari Zone; Coin Exchange (Celadon City)
Description: The female's horn develops slowly. Prefers physical attacks such as clawing and biting.

Learned Skill List:

Level	Skill	Type
—	Growl	Normal
—	Tackle	Normal
—	Scratch	Normal
LV 14	Poison Sting	Poison
LV 23	Tail Whip	Normal
LV 32	Bite	Normal
LV 41	Fury Swipes	Normal
LV 50	Double Kick	Fighting

Technical Machines: 06, 07, 08, 09, 10, 11, 12, 13, 14, 20, 24, 25, 31, 32, 33, 34, 40, 44, 50
Hidden Machines: N/A

Nidoqueen—No. 31

Evolution: Final Form

Vital Statistics
Type: Poison/Ground
Height: 4'3" Weight: 132 lbs
Appearance: —
Description: Its hard scales provide strong protection, and it uses its hefty bulk to execute powerful moves.

Learned Skill List:

Level	Skill	Type
—	Tackle	Normal
—	Scratch	Normal
—	Tail Whip	Normal
LV 14	Poison Sting	Poison
LV 23	Body Slam	Normal

Technical Machines: 01, 05, 06, 07, 08, 09, 10, 11, 12, 13, 14, 15, 16, 17, 18, 19, 20, 24, 25, 26, 27, 31, 32, 33, 34, 38, 40, 44, 48, 50
Hidden Machines: 03, 04

Nidoran ♂—No. 32

Evolution: No. 33 Nidorino (LV 16), Nidoking (Moon Stone)

Vital Statistics
Type: Poison
Height: 1'8" Weight: 20 lbs
Appearance: Route 22 and the Safari Zone
Description: Stiffens its ears to sense danger. The larger its horns, the more powerful its secreted venom.

Learned Skill List:

Level	Skill	Type
—	Leer	Normal
—	Tackle	Normal
LV 8	Horn Attack	Normal
LV 14	Poison Sting	Poison
LV 21	Focus Energy	Normal
LV 29	Fury Attack	Normal
LV 36	Horn Drill	Normal
LV 43	Double Kick	Fighting

Technical Machines: 06, 07, 08, 09, 10, 14, 20, 24, 25, 31, 32, 33, 34, 40, 44, 50
Hidden Machines: N/A

Nidorino—No. 33

Evolution: Nidoking (Moon Stone)

Vital Statistics
Type: Poison
Height: 2'11" Weight: 43 lbs
Appearance: Safari Zone; Coin Exchange (Celadon City)
Description: An aggressive Pokémon that is quick to attack. The horn on its head secretes a powerful venom.

Learned Skill List:

Level	Skill	Type
—	Leer	Normal
—	Tackle	Normal
—	Horn Attack	Normal
LV 14	Poison Sting	Poison
LV 23	Focus Energy	Normal
LV 32	Fury Attack	Normal
LV 41	Horn Drill	Normal
LV 50	Double Kick	Fighting

Technical Machines: 06, 07, 08, 09, 10, 11, 12, 13, 14, 20, 24, 25, 31, 32, 33, 34, 40, 44, 50
Hidden Machines: N/A

Nidoking—No. 34

Evolution: Final Form

Vital Statistics
Type: Poison/Ground
Height: 4'7" Weight: 137 lbs
Appearance: —
Description: It uses its powerful tail in battle to smash, constrict, then break its prey's bones.

Learned Skill List:

Level	Skill	Type
—	Tackle	Normal
—	Horn Attack	Normal
—	Poison Sting	Poison
LV 23	Thrash	Normal

Technical Machines: 01, 05, 06, 07, 08, 09, 10, 11, 12, 13, 14, 15, 16, 17, 18, 19, 20, 24, 25, 26, 27, 31, 32, 33, 34, 38, 40, 44, 48, 50
Hidden Machines: 03, 04

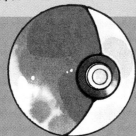

Clefairy—No. 35

Evolution: No. 36 Clefable (Moon Stone)

Vital Statistics
Type: Normal
Height: 2'0" **Weight:** 17 lbs
Appearance: Mt. Moon, Coin Exchange (Celadon City)
Description: Its cute magical appeal brings it many admirers. The Clefairy is rare and found only in certain areas.

Learned Skill List:

Level	Skill	Type
—	Pound	Normal
—	Growl	Normal
LV 13	Sing	Normal
LV 18	Double Slap	Normal
LV 24	Minimize	Normal
LV 31	Metronome	Normal
LV 39	Defense Curl	Normal
LV 43	Light Screen	Psychic

Technical Machines: 01, 05, 06, 08, 09, 10, 11, 12, 13, 14, 17, 18, 19, 20, 22, 24, 25, 29, 30, 31, 32, 33, 34, 35, 38, 40, 44, 45, 46, 49, 50
Hidden Machines: 04, 05

Clefable—No. 36

Evolution: Final Form

Vital Statistics
Type: Normal
Height: 4'3" **Weight:** 88 lbs
Appearance: —
Description: A timid fairy Pokémon that is rarely seen, the Clefable runs and hides the moment it senses people.

Learned Skill List:

Level	Skill	Type
—	Sing	Normal
—	Double Slap	Normal
—	Minimize	Normal
—	Metronome	Normal

Technical Machines: 01, 05, 06, 08, 09, 10, 11, 12, 13, 14, 15, 17, 18, 19, 20, 22, 24, 25, 29, 30, 31, 32, 33, 34, 35, 38, 40, 44, 45, 46, 49, 50
Hidden Machines: 04, 05

Vulpix—No. 37

Evolution: No. 38. Ninetales (Fire Stone)

Vital Statistics
Type: Flame
Height: 2'0" **Weight:** 22 lbs
Appearance: Routes 7 and 8 and the Pokémon House (Cinnabar Island)
Description: At the time of birth it has just one tail, but it splits from the tip as it grows older.

Learned Skill List:

Level	Skill	Type
—	Ember	Flame
—	Tail Whip	Normal
LV 16	Quick Attack	Normal
LV 21	Roar	Normal
LV 28	Confuse Ray	Ghost
LV 35	Flamethrower	Flame
LV 42	Fire Spin	Flame

Technical Machines: 06, 08, 09, 10, 20, 28, 31, 32, 33, 34, 38, 39, 40, 44, 50
Hidden Machines: N/A

Ninetales—No. 38

Evolution: Final Form

Vital Statistics
Type: Flame
Height: 3'7" **Weight:** 44 lbs
Appearance: —
Description: Very smart and very vengeful. Grabbing one of the Ninetales' many tales could result in a 1,000-year curse.

Learned Skill List:

Level	Skill	Type
—	Ember	Flame
—	Tail Whip	Normal
—	Quick Attack	Normal
—	Roar	Normal

Technical Machines: 06, 08, 09, 10, 15, 20, 28, 31, 32, 33, 34, 38, 39, 40, 44, 50
Hidden Machines: N/A

Jigglypuff—No. 39

Evolution: No. 40. Wigglytuff (Moon Stone)

Vital Statistics
Type: Normal
Height: 1'8" **Weight:** 12 lbs
Appearance: Route 3
Description: When its huge eyes light up, the Jigglypuff sings a mysteriously soothing melody that lulls its enemies to sleep.

Learned Skill List:

Level	Skill	Type
—	Sing	Normal
LV 9	Pound	Normal
LV 14	Disable	Normal
LV 19	Defense Curl	Normal
LV 24	Double Slap	Normal
LV 29	Rest	Psychic
LV 34	Body Slam	Normal
LV 39	Double Edge	Normal

Technical Machines: 01, 05, 06, 08, 09, 10, 11, 12, 13, 14, 17, 18, 19, 20, 22, 24, 25, 29, 30, 31, 32, 33, 34, 38, 40, 44, 45, 46, 49, 50
Hidden Machines: 04, 05

Wigglytuff—No. 40

Evolution: Final Form

Vital Statistics
Type: Normal
Height: 3'3" **Weight:** 26 lbs
Appearance: Unknown Dungeon
Description: The Wigglytuff's body is soft and rubbery. When angry, it will suck in air and inflate itself to an enormous size.

Learned Skill List:

Level	Skill	Type
—	Sing	Normal
—	Disable	Normal
—	Defense Curl	Normal
—	Double Slap	Normal

Technical Machines: 01, 05, 06, 08, 09, 10, 11, 12, 13, 14, 15, 17, 18, 19, 20, 22, 24, 25, 29, 30, 31, 32, 33, 34, 38, 40, 44, 45, 46, 49, 50
Hidden Machines: 04, 05

Zubat—No. 41

Evolution: No. 42. Golbat (LV 22)

Vital Statistics
Type: Poison/Flying
Height: 2'7" **Weight:** 17 lbs
Appearance: Mt. Moon, Rock Tunnel, Seafoam Islands, and Victory Road
Description: Forms colonies in perpetually dark places and uses ultrasonic waves to identify and approach targets.

Learned Skill List:

Level	Skill	Type
—	Leech Life	Bug
LV 10	Supersonic	Normal
LV 15	Bite	Normal
LV 21	Confuse Ray	Ghost
LV 28	Wing Attack	Flying
LV 36	Haze	Ice

Technical Machines: 02, 04, 06, 09, 10, 20, 21, 31, 32, 34, 39, 44, 50
Hidden Machines: N/A

Golbat—No. 42

Evolution: Final Form

Vital Statistics
Type: Poison/Flying
Height: 5'3" **Weight:** 121 lbs
Appearance: Seafoam Islands, Victory Road, and Unknown Dungeon
Description: Once it strikes, it won't stop draining energy from the victim even if it gets too heavy to fly.

Learned Skill List:

Level	Skill	Type
—	Leech Life	Bug
—	Screech	Normal
—	Bite	Normal
LV 21	Confuse Ray	Ghost
LV 28	Wing Attack	Flying
LV 36	Haze	Ice

Technical Machines: 02, 04, 06, 09, 10, 15, 20, 21, 31, 32, 34, 39, 44, 50
Hidden Machines: N/A

Oddish—No. 43

Evolution: No. 44. Gloom (LV 21), Vileplume (Leaf Stone)

Vital Statistics
Type: Grass/Poison
Height: 1'8" **Weight:** 12 lbs
Appearance: Routes 5, 6, 7, 12, 13, 14, 15, 24, and 25
Description: During the day, it keeps its face buried in the ground. At night, it wanders around sowing its seeds.

Learned Skill List:

Level	Skill	Type
—	Absorb	Grass
LV 15	Poison Powder	Poison
LV 17	Stun Spore	Grass
LV 19	Sleep Powder	Grass
LV 24	Acid	Poison
LV 33	Petal Dance	Grass
LV 46	Solarbeam	Grass

Technical Machines: 03, 06, 09, 10, 20, 21, 22, 31, 32, 33, 34, 44, 50
Hidden Machines: 01

Gloom—No. 44

Evolution: Vileplume (Leaf Stone)

Vital Statistics

Type: Grass/Poison
Height: 2'7" Weight: 19 lbs
Appearance: Routes 12, 13, 14, and 15
Description: The fluid that oozes from its mouth isn't saliva, it is a nectar that is used to attract prey.

Learned Skill List:

Level	Skill	Type
—	Absorb	Grass
—	Poison Powder	Poison
—	Stun Spore	Grass
LV 19	Sleep Powder	Grass
LV 28	Acid	Poison
LV 38	Petal Dance	Grass
LV 52	Solarbeam	Grass

Technical Machines: 03, 06, 09, 10, 20, 21, 22, 31, 32, 33, 34, 44, 50
Hidden Machines: 01

Vileplume—No. 45

Evolution: Final Form

Vital Statistics

Type: Grass/Poison
Height: 3'11" Weight: 41 lbs
Appearance: —
Description: The larger its petals, the more toxic pollen it contains. Its big head is heavy and hard to hold up.

Learned Skill List:

Level	Skill	Type
LV 15	Poison Powder	Poison
LV 17	Stun Spore	Grass
LV 19	Sleep Powder	Grass

Technical Machines: 03, 06, 09, 10, 15, 20, 21, 22, 31, 32, 33, 34, 44, 50
Hidden Machines: 01

Paras—No. 46

Evolution: No. 47. Parasect (LV 24)

Vital Statistics

Type: Bug/Grass
Height: 1'0" Weight: 12 lbs
Appearance: Mt. Moon and the Safari Zone
Description: Burrows to suck tree roots. The mushrooms on its back grow by drawing nutrients from the bug host.

Learned Skill List:

Level	Skill	Type
—	Scratch	Normal
LV13	Stun Spore	Grass
LV 20	Leech Life	Bug
LV 27	Spore	Grass
LV 34	Slash	Normal
LV 41	Growth	Normal

Technical Machines: 03, 06, 08, 09, 10, 20, 21, 22, 28, 31, 32, 33, 34, 40, 44, 50
Hidden Machines: 01

Parasect—No. 47

Evolution: Final Form

Vital Statistics

Type: Bug/Grass
Height: 3'3" Weight: 65 lbs
Appearance: The Safari Zone and Unknown Dungeon
Description: A host-parasite pair in which the parasite mushroom has taken over the host bug. Prefers damp places.

Learned Skill List:

Level	Skill	Type
—	Scratch	Normal
—	Stun Spore	Grass
—	Leech Life	Bug
LV 30	Spore	Grass
LV 39	Slash	Normal
LV 48	Growth	Normal

Technical Machines: 03, 06, 08, 09, 10, 15, 20, 21, 22, 28, 31, 32, 33, 34, 40, 44, 50
Hidden Machines: 01

Venonat—No. 48

Evolution: No. 49. Venomoth (LV 31)

Vital Statistics

Type: Bug/Poison
Height: 3'3" Weight: 66 lbs
Appearance: Routes 12, 13, 14, and 15 and the Safari Zone
Description: Lives in the shadows of tall trees, where it eats insects. It is attracted by light at night.

Learned Skill List:

Level	Skill	Type
—	Tackle	Normal
—	Disable	Normal
LV 24	Poison Powder	Poison
LV 27	Leech Life	Bug
LV 30	Stun Spore	Grass
LV 35	Psybeam	Psychic
LV 38	Sleep Powder	Grass
LV 41	Psychic	Psychic

Technical Machines: 06, 09, 10, 20, 21, 22, 29, 31, 32, 33, 34, 44, 46, 50
Hidden Machines: N/A

Venomoth—No. 49

Evolution: Final Form

Vital Statistics

Type: Bug/Poison
Height: 4'11" Weight: 28 lbs
Appearance: The Safari Zone, Victory Road, and Unknown Dungeon
Description: The dust-like scales covering its wings are color coded to indicate the kinds of poison it has.

Learned Skill List:

Level	Skill	Type
—	Tackle	Normal
—	Disable	Normal
—	Poison Powder	Poison
—	Leech Life	Bug
LV 30	Stun Spore	Grass
LV 38	Psybeam	Psychic
LV 43	Sleep Powder	Grass
LV 50	Psychic	Psychic

Technical Machines: 02, 05, 06, 09, 10, 15, 20, 21, 22, 29, 30, 31, 32, 33, 34, 39, 44, 46, 50
Hidden Machines: N/A

Diglett—No. 50

Evolution: No. 51. Dugtrio (LV 26)

Vital Statistics

Type: Ground
Height: 0'8" Weight: 2 lbs
Appearance: Diglett's Cave
Description: Lives about three feet underground, where it feeds on plant roots. It sometimes appears above ground.

Learned Skill List:

Level	Skill	Type
—	Scratch	Normal
LV 15	Growl	Normal
LV 19	Dig	Ground
LV 24	Sand Attack	Normal
LV 31	Slash	Normal
LV 40	Earthquake	Ground

Technical Machines: 06, 08, 09, 10, 20, 26, 27, 28, 31, 32, 34, 44, 48, 50
Hidden Machines: N/A

Dugtrio—No. 51

Evolution: Final Form

Vital Statistics

Type: Ground
Height: 2'4" Weight: 73 lbs
Appearance: Diglett's Cave
Description: A team of Diglett triplets, it triggers huge earthquakes by burrowing 60 miles underground.

Learned Skill List:

Level	Skill	Type
—	Scratch	Normal
—	Growl	Normal
—	Dig	Ground
—	Sand Attack	Normal
LV 35	Slash	Normal
LV 47	Earthquake	Ground

Technical Machines: 06, 08, 09, 10, 15, 20, 26, 27, 28, 31, 32, 34, 44, 48, 50
Hidden Machines: N/A

Meowth—No. 52

Evolution: No. 53. Persian (LV 28)

Vital Statistics

Type: Normal
Height: 1'4" Weight: 9 lbs
Appearance: Routes 5, 6, 7, and 8
Description: Adores circular objects. Wanders the streets each night to look for dropped change.

Learned Skill List:

Level	Skill	Type
—	Scratch	Normal
—	Growl	Normal
LV 12	Bite	Ground
LV 17	Payday	Normal
LV 24	Screech	Normal
LV 33	Fury Swipes	Normal
LV 44	Slash	Normal

Technical Machines: 06, 08, 09, 10, 11, 12, 16, 20, 24, 25, 31, 32, 34, 39, 40, 44, 50
Hidden Machines: N/A

Persian—No. 53

Evolution: **Final Form**

Vital Statistics
Type: **Normal**
Height: **3'3"** Weight: **71 lbs**
Appearance: —
Description: **Although its fur has many admirers, it is tough to raise as a pet because of its fickle meanness.**

Learned Skill List:

Level	Skill	Type
—	Scratch	Normal
—	Growl	Normal
—	Bite	Ground
—	Payday	Normal
—	Screech	Normal
LV 37	Fury Swipes	Normal
LV 51	Slash	Normal

Technical Machines: 06, 08, 09, 10, 11, 12, 15, 16, 20, 24, 25, 31, 32, 34, 39, 40, 44, 50
Hidden Machines: N/A

Psyduck—No. 54

Evolution: **No. 55. Golduck (LV 33)**

Vital Statistics
Type: **Water**
Height: **2'7"** Weight: **43 lbs**
Appearance: **Routes 4, 24, and 25; Celadon City; Fuchsia City; and Seafoam Islands (by fishing)**
Description: **While lulling its enemies with its vacant look, this wily Pokémon uses its psychokinetic powers.**

Learned Skill List:

Level	Skill	Type
—	Scratch	Normal
LV 28	Tail Whip	Normal
LV 31	Disable	Normal
LV 36	Confusion	Psychic
LV 43	Fury Swipes	Normal
LV 52	Hydro Pump	Water

Technical Machines: 01, 05, 06, 08, 09, 10, 11, 12, 13, 14, 16, 17, 18, 19, 20, 28, 31, 32, 34, 39, 40, 44, 50
Hidden Machines: 03, 04

Golduck—No. 55

Evolution: **Final Form**

Vital Statistics
Type: **Water**
Height: **5'7"** Weight: **169 lbs**
Appearance: **Routes 4, 24, and 25; Celadon City; Fuchsia City; and Seafoam Islands (by fishing)**
Description: **Often seen swimming elegantly by lake shores, it is often mistaken for the Japanese monster, Kappa.**

Learned Skill List:

Level	Skill	Type
—	Scratch	Normal
—	Tail Whip	Normal
—	Disable	Normal
LV 39	Confusion	Psychic
LV 48	Fury Swipes	Normal
LV 59	Hydro Pump	Water

Technical Machines: 01, 05, 06, 08, 09, 10, 11, 12, 13, 14, 15, 16, 17, 18, 19, 20, 28, 31, 32, 34, 39, 40, 44, 50
Hidden Machines: 03, 04

Mankey—No. 56

Evolution: **No. 57. Primeape (LV 28)**

Vital Statistics
Type: **Fighting**
Height: **1'8"** Weight: **62 lbs**
Appearance: **Routes 5, 6, 7, and 8**
Description: **Extremely quick to anger, it can be docile one moment, then angry the next.**

Learned Skill List:

Level	Skill	Type
—	Scratch	Normal
—	Leer	Normal
LV 15	Karate Chop	Normal
LV 21	Fury Swipes	Normal
LV 27	Focus Energy	Normal
LV 33	Seismic Toss	Fighting
LV 39	Thrash	Normal

Technical Machines: 01, 05, 06, 08, 09, 10, 16, 17, 18, 19, 20, 24, 25, 28, 31, 32, 34, 35, 39, 36, 40, 44, 48, 50
Hidden Machines: 04

Primeape—No. 57

Evolution: **Final Form**

Vital Statistics
Type: **Fighting**
Height: **3'3"** Weight: **71 lbs**
Appearance: —
Description: **Always furious and tenacious to boot, it won't abandon a chase until it catches its quarry.**

Learned Skill List:

Level	Skill	Type
—	Scratch	Normal
—	Leer	Normal
—	Karate Chop	Normal
—	Fury Swipes	Normal
LV 27	Focus Energy	Normal
LV 37	Seismic Toss	Fighting
LV 46	Thrash	Normal

Technical Machines: 01, 05, 06, 08, 09, 10, 15, 16, 17, 18, 19, 20, 24, 25, 28, 31, 32, 34, 35, 39, 40, 44, 48, 50
Hidden Machines: 04

Growlithe—No. 58

Evolution: **No. 59. Arcanine (Fire Stone)**

Vital Statistics
Type: **Flame**
Height: **2'4"** Weight: **42 lbs**
Appearance: **Routes 7 and 8 and the Pokémon House (Cinnabar Island)**
Description: **Very protective of its territory, the Growlithe will bark and bite to repel intruders from its space.**

Learned Skill List:

Level	Skill	Type
—	Bite	Normal
—	Roar	Normal
LV 18	Ember	Flame
LV 23	Leer	Normal
LV 30	Take Down	Normal
LV 39	Agility	Psychic
LV 50	Flamethrower	Flame

Technical Machines: 06, 08, 09, 10, 20, 23, 28, 31, 32, 33, 34, 38, 39, 40, 44, 50
Hidden Machines: N/A

Arcanine—No. 59

Evolution: **Final Form**

Vital Statistics
Type: **Flame**
Height: **6'3"** Weight: **342 lbs**
Appearance: —
Description: **A Pokémon that has been admired since the past for its beauty. It runs agilely as if on wings.**

Learned Skill List:

Level	Skill	Type
—	Roar	Normal
—	Ember	Flame
—	Leer	Normal
—	Take Down	Normal

Technical Machines: 06, 08, 09, 10, 15, 20, 23, 28, 30, 31, 32, 33, 34, 38, 39, 40, 44, 50
Hidden Machines: N/A

Poliwag—No. 60

Evolution: **No 61 Poliwhirl (LV 25), No. 62 Poliwrath (Water Stone)**

Vital Statistics
Type: **Water**
Height: **2'0"** Weight: **27 lbs**
Appearance: **Viridian City and Route 22 (by fishing)**
Description: **Its newly grown legs prevent it from running. It prefers swimming to standing.**

Learned Skill List:

Level	Skill	Type
—	Bubble	Water
LV 16	Hypnosis	Psychic
LV 19	Water Gun	Water
LV 25	Double Slap	Normal
LV 31	Body Slam	Normal
LV 38	Amnesia	Psychic
LV 45	Hydro Pump	Water

Technical Machines: 06, 08, 09, 10, 11, 12, 13, 14, 20, 29, 31, 32, 34, 40, 44, 46, 50
Hidden Machines: 03

Poliwhirl—No. 61

Evolution: **No. 62 Poliwrath (Water Stone)**

Vital Statistics
Type: **Water**
Height: **3'3"** Weight: **44 lbs**
Appearance: **Celadon City and Route 10 (by fishing)**
Description: **Capable of living in or out of water. When out of the water, the Poliwhirl sweats to keep its body slimy.**

Learned Skill List:

Level	Skill	Type
—	Bubble	Water
LV 16	Hypnosis	Psychic
LV 19	Water Gun	Water
LV 26	Double Slap	Normal
LV 33	Body Slam	Normal
LV 41	Amnesia	Psychic
LV 49	Hydro Pump	Water

Technical Machines: 01, 05, 06, 08, 09, 10, 11, 12, 13, 14, 17, 18, 19, 20, 26, 27, 29, 31, 32, 34, 35, 40, 44, 46, 50
Hidden Machines: 03, 04

Poliwrath—No. 62

Evolution: Final Form

Vital Statistics
Type: Water/Fighting
Height: 4'3" **Weight:** 119 lbs
Appearance: —
Description: An adept swimmer at the front crawl and breast stroke, the Poliwrath easily overtakes the best human swimmers.

Learned Skill List:

Level	Skill	Type
—	Double Slap	Normal
—	Body Slam	Normal
LV 16	Hypnosis	Psychic
LV 19	Water Gun	Water

Technical Machines: 01, 05, 06, 08, 09, 10, 11, 12, 13, 14, 15, 17, 18, 19, 20, 26, 27, 29, 31, 32, 34, 35, 40, 44, 46, 50
Hidden Machines: 03, 04

Abra—No. 63

Evolution: No. 64 Kadabra (LV 16), No 65 Alakazam (Trade)

Vital Statistics
Type: Psychic
Height: 2'11" **Weight:** 43 lbs
Appearance: Routes 24 and 25; Coin Exchange (Celadon City)
Description: Using its ability to read minds, the Abra identifies impending danger and teleports to safety.

Learned Skill List:

Level	Skill	Type
—	Teleport	Psychic

Technical Machines: 01, 05, 06, 08, 09, 10, 17, 18, 19, 20, 29, 30, 31, 32, 33, 34, 35, 40, 44, 45, 46, 49, 50
Hidden Machines: 05

Kadabra—No. 64

Evolution: No. 65 Alakazam (Trade)

Vital Statistics
Type: Psychic
Height: 4'3" **Weight:** 125 lbs
Appearance: Unknown Dungeon
Description: The Kadabra emits special alpha waves from its body that induce headaches just from being close by.

Learned Skill List:

Level	Skill	Type
—	Teleport	Psychic
LV 16	Confusion	Psychic
LV 20	Disable	Normal
LV 27	Psybeam	Psychic
LV 31	Recover	Normal
LV 38	Psychic	Psychic
LV 42	Reflect	Psychic

Technical Machines: 01, 05, 06, 08, 09, 10, 17, 18, 19, 20, 28, 29, 30, 31, 32, 33, 34, 35, 40, 44, 45, 46, 49, 50
Hidden Machines: 05

Alakazam—No. 65

Evolution: Final Form

Vital Statistics
Type: Psychic
Height: 4'11" **Weight:** 106 lbs
Appearance: —
Description: The Alakazam brain can outperform a supercomputer. Its IQ is said to be 5,000.

Learned Skill List:

Level	Skill	Type
—	Teleport	Psychic
LV 16	Confusion	Psychic
LV 20	Disable	Normal
LV 27	Psybeam	Psychic
LV 31	Recover	Normal
LV 38	Psychic	Psychic
LV 42	Reflect	Psychic

Technical Machines: 01, 05, 06, 08, 09, 10, 15, 17, 18, 19, 20, 29, 30, 31, 32, 33, 34, 35, 40, 44, 45, 46, 49, 50
Hidden Machines: 05

Machop—No. 66

Evolution: No. 67 Machoke (LV 28), No 68 Machamp (Trade)

Vital Statistics
Type: Fighting
Height: 2'7" **Weight:** 43 lbs
Appearance: Rock Tunnel and Victory Road
Description: Loves to build its muscles. The Machop trains in all styles of martial arts to become stronger.

Learned Skill List:

Level	Skill	Type
—	Karate Chop	Normal
LV 20	Low Kick	Fighting
LV 25	Leer	Normal
LV 32	Focus Energy	Normal
LV 39	Seismic Toss	Fighting
LV 46	Submission	Fighting

Technical Machines: 01, 05, 06, 08, 09, 10, 17, 18, 19, 20, 26, 27, 28, 31, 32, 34, 35, 38, 40, 44, 48, 50
Hidden Machines: 04

Machoke—No. 67

Evolution: No 68 Machamp (Trade)

Vital Statistics
Type: Fighting
Height: 4'11" **Weight:** 155 lbs
Appearance: Rock Tunnel and Victory Road
Description: The Machoke's muscular body is so powerful that it must wear a power-save belt to regulate its motions.

Learned Skill List:

Level	Skill	Type
—	Karate Chop	Normal
—	Low Kick	Fighting
—	Leer	Normal
LV 36	Focus Energy	Normal
LV 44	Seismic Toss	Fighting
LV 52	Submission	Fighting

Technical Machines: 01, 05, 06, 08, 09, 10, 17, 18, 19, 20, 26, 27, 28, 31, 32, 34, 35, 38, 40, 44, 48, 50
Hidden Machines: 04

Machamp—No. 68

Evolution: Final Form

Vital Statistics
Type: Fighting
Height: 5'3" **Weight:** 287 lbs
Appearance: Rock Tunnel and Victory Road
Description: Using its heavy muscles, the Machamp throws powerful punches that can send the victim clear over the horizon.

Learned Skill List:

Level	Skill	Type
—	Karate Chop	Normal
—	Low Kick	Fighting
—	Leer	Normal
LV 32	Focus Energy	Normal
LV 39	Seismic Toss	Fighting
LV 46	Submission	Fighting

Technical Machines: 01, 05, 06, 08, 09, 10, 15, 17, 18, 19, 20, 26, 27, 28, 31, 32, 34, 35, 38, 40, 44, 48, 50
Hidden Machines: 04

Bellsprout—No. 69

Evolution: No. 70 Weepinbell (LV 21), No 71 Victreebel (Leaf Stone)

Vital Statistics
Type: Grass/Poison
Height: 2'4" **Weight:** 9 lbs
Appearance: Routes 5, 6, 7, 12, 13, 14, 15, 24 and 25
Description: A carnivorous Pokémon that traps and eats bugs. It uses its root feet to soak up needed moisture.

Learned Skill List:

Level	Skill	JType
—	Vine Whip	Grass
—	Growth	Normal
LV 13	Wrap	Normal
LV 15	Poison Powder	Poison
LV 18	Sleep Powder	Grass
LV 21	Stun Spore	Grass
LV 26	Acid	Poison
LV 33	Razor Leaf	Grass
LV 42	Slam	Normal

Technical Machines: 03, 06, 09, 10, 20, 21, 22, 31, 32, 33, 34, 44, 50
Hidden Machines: 01

Weepinbell—No. 70

Evolution: No 71 Victreebel (Leaf Stone)

Vital Statistics
Type: Grass/Poison
Height: 3'3" **Weight:** 14 lbs
Appearance: Routes 12, 13, 14, and 15
Description: The Weepinbell spits out poison powder to immobilize the enemy, then finishes it with a spray of acid.

Learned Skill List:

Level	Skill	Type
—	Vine Whip	Grass
—	Growth	Normal
—	Wrap	Normal
LV 15	Poison Powder	Poison
LV 18	Sleep Powder	Grass
LV 23	Stun Spore	Grass
LV 29	Acid	Poison
LV 38	Razor Leaf	Grass
LV 49	Slam	Normal

Technical Machines: 03, 06, 09, 10, 20, 21, 22, 31, 32, 33, 34, 44, 50
Hidden Machines: 01

Victreebel—No. 71

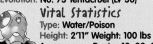

Evolution: Final Form

Vital Statistics
Type: Grass/Poison
Height: 5'7" Weight: 34 lbs
Appearance: —
Description: The Victreebel is said to live in huge colonies deep in jungles, although no one has ever returned from there.

Learned Skill List:

Level	Skill	Type
LV 13	Wrap	Normal
LV 15	Poison Powder	Poison
LV 18	Sleep Powder	Grass

Technical Machines: 03, 06, 08, 09, 10, 15, 20, 21, 22, 31, 32, 33, 34, 44, 50
Hidden Machines: 01

Tentacool—No. 72

Evolution: No. 73 Tentacruel (LV 30)

Vital Statistics
Type: Water/Poison
Height: 2'11" Weight: 100 lbs
Appearance: Routes 19, 20, 21; Pallet Town; Viridian City; and Routes 12, 13, 17, 18 (by fishing)
Description: Drifts in shallow seas. Anglers who hook them by accident are often stung.

Learned Skill List:

Level	Skill	Type
—	Acid	Poison
LV 7	Supersonic	Normal
LV 13	Wrap	Normal
LV 18	Poison Sting	Poison
LV 22	Water Gun	Water
LV 27	Constrict	Normal
LV 33	Barrier	Psychic
LV 40	Screech	Normal
LV 48	Hydro Pump	Water

Technical Machines: 03, 06, 09, 10, 11, 12, 13, 14, 20, 21, 31, 32, 33, 34, 40, 44, 50
Hidden Machines: 01, 03

Tentacruel—No. 73

Evolution: Final Form

Vital Statistics
Type: Water/Poison
Height: 5'3" Weight: 121 lbs
Appearance: —
Description: The Tentacruel's tentacles are normally kept short, but on hunts they're extended to ensnare and immobilize prey.

Learned Skill List:

Level	Skill	Type
—	Acid	Poison
—	Supersonic	Normal
—	Wrap	Normal
LV 18	Poison Sting	Poison
LV 22	Water Gun	Water
LV 27	Constrict	Normal
LV 33	Barrier	Psychic
LV 40	Screech	Normal
LV 48	Hydro Pump	Water

Technical Machines: 03, 06, 09, 10, 11, 12, 13, 14, 15, 20, 21, 31, 32, 33, 34, 40, 44, 50
Hidden Machines: 01, 03

Geodude—No. 74

Evolution: No. 75 Graveler (LV 25), No. 76 Golem (Trade)

Vital Statistics
Type: Rock/Ground
Height: 1'4" Weight: 44 lbs
Appearance: Mt. Moon, Rock Tunnel, Victory Road
Description: Found in fields and mountains, people often step on or trip over them, mistaking them for boulders.

Learned Skill List:

Level	Skill	Type
—	Tackle	Normal
LV 11	Defense Curl	Normal
LV 16	Rock Throw	Rock
LV 21	Self Destruct	Normal
LV 26	Harden	Normal
LV 31	Earthquake	Ground
LV 36	Explosion	Normal

Technical Machines: 01, 06, 08, 09, 10, 17, 18, 19, 20, 26, 27, 28, 31, 32, 34, 35, 36, 38, 44, 47, 48, 50
Hidden Machines: 04

Graveler—No. 75

Evolution: No. 76 Golem (Trade)

Vital Statistics
Type: Rock/Ground
Height: 3'3" Weight: 232 lbs
Appearance: Victory Road
Description: Rolls down slopes to move. The Graveler rolls over any obstacle without slowing or changing its direction.

Learned Skill List:

Level	Skill	Type
—	Tackle	Normal
—	Defense Curl	Normal
LV 16	Rock Throw	Rock
LV 21	Self Destruct	Normal
LV 29	Harden	Normal
LV 36	Earthquake	Ground
LV 43	Explosion	Normal

Technical Machines: 01, 06, 08, 09, 10, 17, 18, 19, 20, 26, 27, 28, 31, 32, 34, 35, 36, 38, 44, 47, 48, 50
Hidden Machines: 04

Golem—No. 76

Evolution: Final Form

Vital Statistics
Type: Rock/Ground
Height: 4'7" Weight: 622 lbs
Appearance: —
Description: Its boulder-like body is extremely hard and can easily withstand dynamite blasts without damage.

Learned Skill List:

Level	Skill	Type
—	Tackle	Normal
—	Defense Curl	Normal
LV 16	Rock Throw	Rock
LV 21	Self Destruct	Normal
LV 29	Harden	Normal
LV 36	Earthquake	Ground
LV 43	Explosion	Normal

Technical Machines: 01, 05, 06, 08, 09, 10, 15, 17, 18, 19, 20, 26, 27, 28, 31, 32, 34, 35, 36, 38, 44, 47, 48, 50
Hidden Machines: 04

Ponyta—No. 77

Evolution: No. 78 Rapidash (LV 40)

Vital Statistics
Type: Flame
Height: 3'3" Weight: 66 lbs
Appearance: Pokémon House (Cinnabar Island)
Description: Its hooves are 10 times harder than diamonds, and it can trample anything completely flat in little time.

Learned Skill List:

Level	Skill	Type
—	Ember	Flame
LV 30	Tail Whip	Normal
LV 32	Stomp	Normal
LV 35	Growl	Normal
LV 39	Fire Spin	Flame
LV 43	Take Down	Normal
LV 48	Agility	Psychic

Technical Machines: 06, 07, 08, 09, 10, 20, 31, 32, 33, 34, 38, 39, 40, 44, 50
Hidden Machines: N/A

Rapidash—No. 78

Evolution: Final Form

Vital Statistics
Type: Flame
Height: 5'7" Weight: 209 lbs
Appearance: —
Description: Very competitive, this Pokémon will chase anything that moves fast in the hopes of racing it.

Learned Skill List:

Level	Skill	Type
—	Ember	Flame
—	Tail Whip	Normal
—	Stomp	Normal
—	Growl	Normal
LV 39	Fire Spin	Flame
LV 47	Take Down	Normal
LV 55	Agility	Psychic

Technical Machines: 06, 07, 08, 09, 10, 15, 20, 31, 32, 33, 34, 38, 39, 40, 44, 50
Hidden Machines: N/A

Slowpoke—No. 79

Evolution: No. 80 Slowbro (LV 37)

Vital Statistics
Type: Water/Psychic
Height: 3'11" Weight: 79 lbs
Appearance: Celadon City, Safari Zone, Seafoam Islands, and Route 10 (by fishing)
Description: Incredibly slow and dopey, it takes five seconds for it to feel pain when under attack.

Learned Skill List:

Level	Skill	Type
—	Confusion	Psychic
LV 18	Disable	Normal
LV 22	Headbutt	Normal
LV 27	Growl	Normal
LV 33	Water Gun	Water
LV 40	Amnesia	Psychic
LV 48	Psychic	Psychic

Technical Machines: 06, 08, 09, 10, 11, 12, 13, 14, 16, 20, 26, 27, 28, 29, 30, 31, 32, 33, 34, 38, 39, 40, 44, 45, 46, 49, 50
Hidden Machines: 03, 04, 05

Slowbro—No. 80

Evolution: Final Form

Vital Statistics

Type: Water/Psychic
Height: 5'3" Weight: 173 lbs
Appearance: Seafoam Islands, Route 23, and Unknown Dungeon
Description: The Shellder that is latched onto the Slowbro's tail is said to feed on the host's leftover scraps.

Learned Skill List:

Level	Skill	Type
—	Confusion	Psychic
—	Disable	Normal
—	Headbutt	Normal
—	Growl	Normal
—	Water Gun	Water
LV 37	Withdraw	Water
LV 44	Amnesia	Psychic
LV 55	Psychic	Psychic

Technical Machines: 01, 05, 06, 08, 09, 10, 11, 12, 13, 14, 15, 16, 17, 18, 19, 20, 26, 27, 28, 29, 30, 31, 32, 33, 34, 38, 39, 40, 44, 45, 46, 49, 50
Hidden Machines: 03, 04, 05

Magnemite—No. 81

Evolution: No. 82 Magneton (LV 30)

Vital Statistics

Type: Electric
Height: 1'0" Weight: 13 lbs
Appearance: Power Plant
Description: Uses anti-gravity to stay suspended in air. Appears without warning and uses Thunder Wave and similar moves.

Learned Skill List:

Level	Skill	Type
—	Tackle	Normal
LV 21	Sonicboom	Normal
LV 25	Thundershock	Electric
LV 29	Supersonic	Normal
LV 35	Thunder Wave	Electric
LV 41	Swift	Normal
LV 47	Screech	Normal

Technical Machines: 06, 09, 10, 20, 24, 25, 30, 31, 32, 33, 34, 39, 44, 45, 50
Hidden Machines: N/A

Magneton—No. 82

Evolution: Final Form

Vital Statistics

Type: Electric
Height: 3'3" Weight: 132 lbs
Appearance: Power Plant, Unknown Dungeon
Description: Formed by several Magnemites linked together. They frequently appear when sunspots flare up.

Learned Skill List:

Level	Skill	Type
—	Tackle	Normal
—	Sonicboom	Normal
—	Thundershock	Electric
—	Supersonic	Normal
LV 38	Thunder Wave	Electric
LV 46	Swift	Normal
LV 54	Screech	Normal

Technical Machines: 06, 09, 10, 20, 24, 25, 30, 31, 32, 33, 34, 39, 44, 45, 50
Hidden Machines: N/A

Farfetch'd—No. 83

Evolution: Final Form

Vital Statistics

Type: Normal/Flying
Height: 2'7" Weight: 33 lbs
Appearance: Vermilion City
Description: The sprig of green onions it holds is its weapon. It is used much like a metal sword.

Learned Skill List:

Level	Skill	Type
—	Peck	Flying
—	Sand Attack	Normal
LV 7	Leer	Normal
LV 15	Fury Attack	Normal
LV 23	Swords Dance	Normal
LV 31	Agility	Psychic
LV 39	Slash	Normal

Technical Machines: 02, 03, 04, 06, 08, 09, 10, 20, 31, 32, 33, 34, 39, 40, 44, 50
Hidden Machines: 01, 02

Doduo—No. 84

Evolution: No. 85 Dodrio (LV 31)

Vital Statistics

Type: Normal/Flying
Height: 4'7" Weight: 86 lbs
Appearance: Routes 16, 17, 18 and the Safari Zone
Description: A bird that makes up for its poor flying with its fast foot speed. Leaves giant footprints.

Learned Skill List:

Level	Skill	Type
—	Peck	Flying
LV 20	Growl	Normal
LV 24	Fury Attack	Normal
LV 30	Drill Peck	Flying
LV 36	Rage	Normal
LV 40	Tri-Attack	Normal
LV 44	Agility	Psychic

Technical Machines: 04, 06, 08, 09, 10, 20, 31, 32, 33, 34, 40, 43, 44, 49, 50
Hidden Machines: 02

Dodrio—No. 85

Evolution: Final Form

Vital Statistics

Type: Normal/Flying
Height: 5'11" Weight: 188 lbs
Appearance: Unknown Dungeon
Description: Uses its three brains to execute complex plans. While two heads sleep, one head stays awake.

Learned Skill List:

Level	Skill	Type
—	Peck	Flying
—	Growl	Normal
—	Fury Attack	Normal
—	Drill Peck	Flying
LV 36	Rage	Normal
LV 40	Tri Attack	Normal
LV 44	Agility	Psychic

Technical Machines: 04, 06, 08, 09, 10, 15, 20, 31, 32, 33, 34, 40, 43, 44, 49, 50
Hidden Machines: 02

Seel—No. 86

Evolution: No. 87 Dewgong (LV 34)

Vital Statistics

Type: Water
Height: 3'7" Weight: 198 lbs
Appearance: Seafoam Islands
Description: The protruding horn on its head is very hard and is used for bashing through thick ice.

Learned Skill List:

Level	Skill	Type
—	Headbutt	Normal
LV 30	Growl	Normal
LV 35	Aurora Beam	Ice
LV 40	Rest	Psychic
LV 45	Take Down	Normal
LV 50	Ice Beam	Ice

Technical Machines: 06, 07, 08, 09, 10, 11, 12, 13, 14, 16, 20, 31, 32, 34, 40, 44, 50
Hidden Machines: 03, 04

Dewgong—No. 87

Evolution: Final Form

Vital Statistics

Type: Water/Ice
Height: 5'7" Weight: 265 lbs
Appearance: Seafoam Islands
Description: Stores thermal energy in its body. Swims at a steady eight knots even in intensely cold waters.

Learned Skill List:

Level	Skill	Type
—	Headbutt	Normal
—	Growl	Normal
LV 35	Aurora Beam	Ice
LV 44	Rest	Psychic
LV 50	Take Down	Normal
LV 56	Ice Beam	Ice

Technical Machines: 06, 07, 08, 09, 10, 11, 12, 13, 14, 15, 16, 20, 31, 32, 34, 40, 44, 50
Hidden Machines: 03, 04

Grimer—No. 88

Evolution: No. 89 Muk (LV 38)

Vital Statistics

Type: Poison
Height: 2'11" Weight: 66 lbs
Appearance: Pokémon House (Cinnabar Island)
Description: Appears in filthy areas and thrives by sucking up polluted sludge that is pumped out of factories.

Learned Skill List:

Level	Skill	Type
—	Pound	Normal
—	Disable	Normal
LV 30	Poison Gas	Poison
LV 33	Minimize	Normal
LV 37	Sludge	Poison
LV 42	Harden	Normal
LV 48	Screech	Normal
LV 55	Acid Armor	Poison

Technical Machines: 06, 08, 20, 21, 24, 25, 31, 32, 34, 36, 38, 44, 47, 50
Hidden Machines: N/A

Muk—No. 89

Evolution: Final Form

Vital Statistics
Type: Poison
Height: 3'11" **Weight:** 66 lbs
Appearance: Pokémon House (Cinnabar Island)
Description: Thickly covered with a filthy, vile sludge. It is so toxic, even its footprints contain poison.

Learned Skill List:

Level	Skill	Type
—	Pound	Normal
—	Disable	Normal
—	Poison Gas	Poison
—	Minimize	Normal
—	Sludge	Poison
LV 42	Harden	Normal
LV 48	Screech	Normal
LV 55	Acid Armor	Poison

Technical Machines: 06, 08, 15, 20, 21, 24, 25, 31, 32, 34, 36, 38, 44, 47, 50
Hidden Machines: N/A

Shellder—No. 90

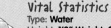

Evolution: No. 91 Cloyster (Water Stone)

Vital Statistics
Type: Water
Height: 1'0" **Weight:** 9 lbs
Appearance: Routes 6, 11, Vermilion City, Cerulean City, and Seafoam Island (by fishing)
Description: Its hard shell repels any kind of attack. It's vulnerable only when its shell is open.

Learned Skill List:

Level	Skill	Type
—	Tackle	Normal
—	Withdraw	Water
LV 18	Supersonic	Normal
LV 23	Clamp	Water
LV 30	Aurora Beam	Ice
LV 39	Leer	Normal
LV 50	Ice Beam	Ice

Technical Machines: 06, 09, 10, 11, 12, 13, 14, 20, 30, 31, 32, 33, 34, 36, 39, 44, 47, 49, 50
Hidden Machines: 03

Cloyster—No. 91

Evolution: Final Form

Vital Statistics
Type: Water/Ice
Height: 4'11" **Weight:** 292 lbs
Appearance: —
Description: When attacked, it launches its horns in quick volleys. The Cloyster's innards have never been seen.

Learned Skill List:

Level	Skill	Type
—	Withdraw	Water
—	Supersonic	Normal
—	Clamp	Water
—	Aurora Beam	Ice
LV 50	Spike Cannon	Normal

Technical Machines: 06, 09, 10, 11, 12, 13, 14, 15, 20, 30, 31, 32, 33, 34, 36, 39, 44, 47, 49, 50
Hidden Machines: 03

Gastly—No. 92

Evolution: No. 93 Hauter (LV 25), No. 94 Gengar (Trade)

Vital Statistics
Type: Ghost/Poison
Height: 4'3" **Weight:** 0.2 lbs
Appearance: Pokémon Tower (Lavender Town)
Description: Almost invisible, this gaseous Pokémon cloaks the target and puts it to sleep without notice.

Learned Skill List:

Level	Skill	Type
—	Lick	Ghost
—	Confuse Ray	Ghost
—	Nightshade	Ghost
LV 27	Hypnosis	Psychic
LV 35	Dream Eater	Psychic

Technical Machines: 06, 20, 21, 24, 25, 29, 31, 32, 34, 36, 42, 44, 46, 47, 50
Hidden Machines: N/A

Haunter—No. 93

Evolution: No. 94 Gengar (Trade)

Vital Statistics
Type: Ghost/Poison
Height: 5'3" **Weight:** 0.2 lbs
Appearance: Pokémon Tower (Lavender Town)
Description: Because of its ability to slip through block walls, it is said to be from another dimension.

Learned Skill List:

Level	Skill	Type
—	Lick	Ghost
—	Confuse Ray	Ghost
—	Nightshade	Ghost
LV 29	Hypnosis	Psychic
LV 38	Dream Eater	Psychic

Technical Machines: 06, 20, 21, 24, 25, 29, 31, 32, 34, 36, 42, 44, 46, 47, 50
Hidden Machines: N/A

Gengar—No. 94

Evolution: Final Form

Vital Statistics
Type: Ghost/Poison
Height: 4'11" **Weight:** 89 lbs
Appearance: —
Description: Under a full moon, this Pokémon likes to mimic the shadows of people and laugh at their fright.

Learned Skill List:

Level	Skill	Type
—	Lick	Ghost
—	Confuse Ray	Ghost
—	Nightshade	Ghost
LV 29	Hypnosis	Psychic
LV 38	Dream Eater	Psychic

Technical Machines: 01, 05, 06, 08, 09, 10, 15, 17, 18, 19, 20, 21, 24, 25, 29, 31, 32, 34, 35, 36, 40, 42, 44, 46, 47, 50
Hidden Machines: 04

Onix—No.95

Evolution: Final Form

Vital Statistics
Type: Rock/Ground
Height: 28'10" **Weight:** 463 lbs
Appearance: Rock Tunnel, Victory Road
Description: As the Onix grows, the stone portions of its body harden to become similar to a diamond but colored black.

Learned Skill List:

Level	Skill	Type
—	Tackle	Normal
—	Screech	Normal
LV 15	Bind	Normal
LV 19	Rock Throw	Rock
LV 25	Rage	Normal
LV 33	Slam	Normal
LV 43	Harden	Normal

Technical Machines: 06, 08, 09, 10, 20, 26, 27, 28, 31, 32, 34, 36, 40, 44, 47, 48, 50
Hidden Machines: 04

Drowsee—No. 96

Evolution: No. 97 Hypno (LV 26)

Vital Statistics
Type: Psychic
Height: 3'3" **Weight:** 71 lbs
Appearance: Route 11
Description: Puts enemies to sleep, then eats their dreams. Occasionally gets sick from eating bad dreams.

Learned Skill List:

Level	Skill	Type
—	Pound	Normal
—	Hypnosis	Psychic
LV 12	Disable	Normal
LV 17	Confusion	Psychic
LV 24	Headbutt	Normal
LV 29	Poison Gas	Poison
LV 32	Psychic	Psychic
LV 37	Meditate	Psychic

Technical Machines: 01, 05, 06, 08, 09, 10, 17, 18, 19, 20, 29, 30, 31, 32, 33, 34, 35, 40, 42, 44, 45, 46, 49, 50
Hidden Machines: 05

Hypno—No 97

Evolution: Final Form

Vital Statistics
Type: Psychic
Height: 5'3" **Weight:** 167 lbs
Appearance: Unknown Dungeon
Description: When it locks eyes with an enemy, it will use a mix of PSI moves such as Hypnosis and Confusion.

Learned Skill List:

Level	Skill	Type
—	Pound	Normal
—	Hypnosis	Psychic
—	Disable	Normal
—	Confusion	Psychic
—	Headbutt	Normal
LV 33	Poison Gas	Poison
LV 37	Psychic	Psychic
LV 43	Meditate	Psychic

Technical Machines: 01, 05, 06, 08, 09, 10, 15, 17, 18, 19, 20, 29, 30, 31, 32, 33, 34, 35, 40, 42, 44, 45, 46, 49, 50
Hidden Machines: 05

Krabby—No. 98

Evolution: No. 99 Kingler (LV 28)

Vital Statistics
Type: Water
Height: 1'4" Weight: 14 lbs
Appearance: Routes 4, 6, 11, 12, 13, 17, 18, 24 and 25, Fuchsia City, Cerulean City, Vermilion City, and the Safari Zone; Seafoam Islands (by fishing)
Description: The Krabby's pincers are not only powerful weapons, they are also used for balance when walking sideways.

Learned Skill List:

Level	Skill	Type
—	Bubble	Water
—	Leer	Normal
LV 20	Vice Grip	Normal
LV 25	Guillotine	Normal
LV 30	Stomp	Normal
LV 35	Crab Hammer	Water
LV 40	Harden	Normal

Technical Machines: 03, 06, 08, 09, 10, 11, 12, 13, 14, 20, 31, 32, 34, 44, 50
Hidden Machines: 01, 03, 04

Kingler—No. 99

Evolution: Final Form

Vital Statistics
Type: Water
Height: 4'3" Weight: 132 lbs
Appearance: Route 23 and Unknown Dungeon. Seafoam Islands (by fishing)
Description: The large pincer has 10,000 HP of crushing power. However, its huge size makes it unwieldy to use.

Learned Skill List:

Level	Skill	Type
—	Bubble	Water
—	Leer	Normal
—	Vice Grip	Normal
LV 25	Guillotine	Normal
LV 34	Stomp	Normal
LV 42	Crab Hammer	Water
LV 49	Harden	Normal

Technical Machines: 03, 06, 08, 09, 10, 11, 12, 13, 14, 15, 20, 31, 32, 34, 44, 50
Hidden Machines: 01, 03, 04

Voltorb—No. 100

Evolution: No. 101 Electrode (LV 30)

Vital Statistics
Type: Electric
Height: 1'8" Weight: 23 lbs
Appearance: Route 10, Power Plant
Description: Usually found in power plants. Easily mistaken for a Poke Ball, they have zapped many people.

Learned Skill List:

Level	Skill	Type
—	Tackle	Normal
—	Screech	Normal
LV 17	Sonicbeam	Normal
LV 22	Self Destruct	Normal
LV 29	Light Screen	Psychic
LV 36	Swift	Normal
LV 43	Explosion	Normal

Technical Machines: 06, 09, 24, 25, 30, 31, 32, 33, 34, 36, 39, 44, 45, 47, 50
Hidden Machines: 05

Electrode—No. 101

Evolution: Final Form

Vital Statistics
Type: Electric
Height: 3'11" Weight: 147 lbs
Appearance: Cerulean Cave
Description: It stores electric energy under very high pressure, and it often explodes with little or no provocation.

Learned Skill List:

Level	Skill	Type
—	Tackle	Normal
—	Screech	Normal
—	Sonicbeam	Normal
LV 22	Self Destruct	Normal
LV 29	Light Screen	Psychic
LV 40	Swift	Normal
LV 50	Explosion	Normal

Technical Machines: 06, 09, 15, 24, 25, 30, 31, 32, 33, 34, 36, 39, 40, 44, 45, 47, 50
Hidden Machines: 05

Exeggcute—No. 102

Evolution: No. 103 Exeggutor (Leaf Stone)

Vital Statistics
Type: Grass/Psychic
Height: 1'4" Weight: 6 lbs
Appearance: Safari Zone
Description: Often mistaken for eggs, when disturbed they quickly gather and attack in swarms.

Learned Skill List:

Level	Skill	Type
—	Barrage	Normal
—	Hypnosis	Psychic
LV 25	Reflect	Psychic
LV 28	Leech Seed	Grass
LV 32	Stun Spore	Grass
LV 37	Poison Powder	Poison
LV 42	Solarbeam	Grass
LV 48	Sleep Powder	Grass

Technical Machines: 06, 09, 10, 20, 29, 30, 31, 32, 33, 34, 36, 37, 44, 46, 47, 50
Hidden Machines: N/A

Exeggutor—No. 103

Evolution: Final Form

Vital Statistics
Type: Grass/Psychic
Height: 6'7" Weight: 265 lbs
Appearance: —
Description: Legend has it that on rare occasions one of its heads will drop off and continue on as an Exeggcute.

Learned Skill List:

Level	Skill	Type
—	Barrage	Normal
—	Hypnosis	Psychic
LV 28	Stomp	Normal

Technical Machines: 06, 09, 10, 15, 20, 21, 22, 29, 30, 31, 32, 33, 34, 36, 37, 44, 46, 47, 50
Hidden Machines: 04

Cubone—No. 104

Evolution: No. 105 Marowak (LV 28)

Vital Statistics
Type: Ground
Height: 1'4" Weight: 14 lbs
Appearance: Pokémon Tower (Lavender Town)
Description: Because the Cubone never removes its skull helmet, no one has ever seen this Pokémon's real face.

Learned Skill List:

Level	Skill	Type
—	Bone Club	Ground
—	Growl	Normal
LV 25	Leer	Normal
LV 31	Focus Energy	Normal
LV 38	Thrash	Normal
LV 43	Bonemerang	Ground
LV 46	Rage	Normal

Technical Machines: 01, 05, 06, 08, 09, 10, 11, 12, 13, 14, 17, 18, 19, 20, 26, 27, 28, 31, 32, 34, 38, 40, 44, 50
Hidden Machines: 04

Marowak—No. 105

Evolution: Final Form

Vital Statistics
Type: Ground
Height: 3'3" Weight: 99 lbs
Appearance: Victory Road, Unknown Dungeon
Description: The bone it holds is its key weapon. The Marowak throws the bone skillfully like a boomerang to KO its targets.

Learned Skill List:

Level	Skill	Type
—	Bone Club	Ground
—	Growl	Normal
—	Leer	Normal
LV 33	Focus Energy	Normal
LV 41	Thrash	Normal
LV 48	Bonemerang	Ground
LV 55	Rage	Normal

Technical Machines: 01, 05, 06, 08, 09, 10, 11, 12, 13, 14, 15, 17, 18, 19, 20, 26, 27, 28, 31, 32, 34, 38, 40, 44, 50
Hidden Machines: 04

Hitmonlee—No. 106

Evolution: Final Form

Vital Statistics
Type: Fighting
Height: 4'11" Weight: 110 lbs
Appearance: Saffron City
Description: When in a hurry, the Hitmonlee's legs lengthen progressively. It runs smoothly with extra long, loping strides.

Learned Skill List:

Level	Skill	Type
—	Double Kick	Fighting
—	Meditate	Psychic
LV 33	Rolling Kick	Fighting
LV 38	Jump Kick	Fighting
LV 43	Focus Energy	Normal
LV 48	High Jump Kick	Fighting
LV 53	Mega Kick	Normal

Technical Machines: 01, 05, 06, 08, 09, 10, 17, 18, 19, 20, 31, 32, 34, 35, 39, 40, 44, 50
Hidden Machines: 04

Hitmonchan—No. 107

Evolution: Final Form

Vital Statistics

Type: Fighting
Height: 4'7" **Weight:** 111 lbs
Appearance: Saffron City
Description: While apparently doing nothing, the Hitmonchan fires punches in lightning fast volleys that are impossible to see.

Learned Skill List:

Level	Skill	Type
—	Comet Punch	Normal
—	Agility	Psychic
LV 33	Fire Punch	Flame
LV 38	Ice Punch	Ice
LV 43	Thunder Punch	Electric
LV 48	Mega Punch	Normal
LV 53	Counter	Fighting

Technical Machines: 01, 05, 06, 08, 09, 10, 17, 18, 19, 20, 31, 32, 34, 35, 39, 40, 44, 50
Hidden Machines: 04

Lickitung—No. 108

Evolution: Final Form

Vital Statistics

Type: Normal
Height: 3'11" **Weight:** 144 lbs
Appearance: Route 18
Description: Its tongue can be extended like a chameleon's and leaves a tingling sensation when it licks.

Learned Skill List:

Level	Skill	Type
—	Wrap	Normal
—	Supersonic	Normal
LV 7	Stomp	Normal
LV 15	Disable	Normal
LV 23	Defense Curl	Normal
LV 31	Slam	Normal
LV 39	Screech	Normal

Technical Machines: 01, 03, 05, 06, 08, 09, 10, 11, 12, 13, 14, 15, 17, 18, 19, 20, 24, 25, 26, 27, 31, 32, 34, 38, 40, 44, 50
Hidden Machines: 01, 03, 04

Koffing—No. 109

Evolution: No. 110 Weezing (LV35)

Vital Statistics

Type: Poison
Height: 2'0" **Weight:** 2 lbs
Appearance: Pokémon House (Cinnabar Island)
Description: Because it stores several kinds of toxic gases in its body, the Koffing is prone to exploding without warning.

Learned Skill List:

Level	Skill	Type
—	Tackle	Normal
—	Smog	Poison
LV 32	Sludge	Poison
LV 37	Smokescreen	Normal
LV 40	Self Destruct	Normal
LV 45	Haze	Ice
LV 48	Explosion	Normal

Technical Machines: 06, 20, 24, 25, 31, 32, 34, 36, 38, 44, 47, 50
Hidden Machines: N/A

Weezing—No. 110

Evolution: Final Form

Vital Statistics

Type: Poison
Height: 3'11" **Weight:** 21 lbs
Appearance: Pokémon House (Cinnabar Island)
Description: Where two kinds of poison gases meet, two Koffings can fuse into a Weezing over many years.

Learned Skill List:

Level	Skill	Type
—	Tackle	Normal
—	Smog	Poison
—	Sludge	Poison
LV 39	Smokescreen	Normal
LV 43	Self Destruct	Normal
LV 49	Haze	Ice
LV 53	Explosion	Normal

Technical Machines: 06, 15, 20, 24, 25, 31, 32, 34, 36, 38, 44, 47, 50
Hidden Machines: N/A

Rhyhorn—No. 111

Evolution: No. 112 Rhydon (LV 42)

Vital Statistics

Type: Ground/Rock
Height: 3'3" **Weight:** 254 lbs
Appearance: Safari Zone
Description: Its massive bones are 1,000 times harder than human bones. The Rhyhorn can easily send something as large as a trailer flying.

Learned Skill List:

Level	Skill	Type
—	Horn Attack	Normal
LV 30	Stomp	Normal
LV 35	Tail Whip	Normal
LV 40	Fury Attack	Normal
LV 45	Horn Drill	Normal
LV 50	Leer	Normal
LV 55	Take Down	Normal

Technical Machines: 06, 07, 08, 09, 10, 20, 24, 25, 26, 27, 28, 31, 32, 34, 38, 40, 44, 48, 50
Hidden Machines: 04

Rhydon—No. 112

Evolution: Final Form

Vital Statistics

Type: Ground/Rock
Height: 6'3" **Weight:** 265 lbs
Appearance: Unknown Dungeon
Description: Protected by an armor-like hide, the Rhydon is capable of living in molten lava of 3,600 degrees.

Learned Skill List:

Level	Skill	Type
—	Horn Attack	Normal
—	Stomp	Normal
—	Tail Whip	Normal
—	Fury Attack	Normal
LV 48	Horn Drill	Normal
LV 55	Leer	Normal
LV 64	Take Down	Normal

Technical Machines: 01, 05, 06, 07, 08, 09, 10, 11, 12, 13, 14, 15, 16, 17, 18, 19, 20, 24, 25, 26, 27, 28, 31, 32, 34, 38, 40, 44, 48, 50
Hidden Machines: 03, 04

Chansey—No. 113

Evolution: Final Form

Vital Statistics

Type: Normal
Height: 3'7" **Weight:** 76 lbs
Appearance: Safari Zone and Unknown Dungeon
Description: A rare and elusive Pokémon that is said to bring happiness to those who manage to get one.

Learned Skill List:

Level	Skill	Type
—	Pound	Normal
—	Double Slap	Normal
LV 24	Sing	Normal
LV 30	Growl	Normal
LV 38	Minimize	Normal
LV 44	Defense Curl	Normal
LV 48	Light Screen	Psychic
LV 54	Double Edge	Normal

Technical Machines: 01, 05, 06, 08, 10, 11, 12, 13, 14, 15, 17, 18, 19, 20, 22, 24, 25, 29, 30, 31, 32, 33, 34, 35, 37, 38, 40, 41, 44, 45, 46, 49, 50
Hidden Machines: 04, 05

Tangela—No. 114

Evolution: Final Form

Vital Statistics

Type: Grass
Height: 3'3" **Weight:** 77 lbs
Appearance: Route 21
Description: The Tangela's whole body is swathed with wide vines that are similar to seaweed. Its vines shake as it walks.

Learned Skill List:

Level	Skill	Type
—	Constrict	Normal
—	Bind	Normal
LV 29	Absorb	Grass
LV 32	Poison Powder	Poison
LV 36	Stun Spore	Grass
LV 39	Sleep Powder	Grass
LV 45	Slam	Normal
LV 49	Growth	Normal

Technical Machines: 03, 06, 08, 09, 10, 15, 20, 21, 22, 31, 32, 34, 40, 44, 50
Hidden Machines: 01

Kangaskhan—No. 115

Evolution: Final Form

Vital Statistics

Type: Normal
Height: 7'3" **Weight:** 176 lbs
Appearance: Safari Zone
Description: The infant rarely ventures out of its mother's protective pouch before it is three years old.

Learned Skill List:

Level	Skill	Type
—	Comet Punch	Normal
—	Rage	Normal
LV 26	Bite	Normal
LV 31	Tail Whip	Normal
LV 36	Mega Punch	Normal
LV 41	Leer	Normal
LV 46	Dizzy Punch	Normal

Technical Machines: 01, 05, 06, 08, 09, 10, 11, 12, 13, 14, 15, 17, 18, 19, 20, 24, 25, 26, 27, 31, 32, 34, 38, 40, 44, 48, 50
Hidden Machines: 03, 04

Horsea—No. 116

Evolution: No. 117 Seadra (LV 32)

Vital Statistics
Type: Water
Height: 1'4" Weight: 18 lbs
Appearance: Cinnabar Island; Routes 19, 20, and 21. Seafoam Islands (by fishing)
Description: Known to shoot down flying bugs with precision blasts of ink from the surface of the water.

Learned Skill List:

Level	Skill	Type
—	Bubble	Water
LV 19	Smokescreen	Normal
LV 24	Leer	Normal
LV 30	Water Gun	Water
LV 37	Agility	Psychic
LV 45	Hydro Pump	Water

Technical Machines: 06, 09, 10, 11, 12, 13, 14, 20, 31, 32, 34, 39, 40, 44, 50
Hidden Machines: 03

Seadra—No. 117

Evolution: Final Form

Vital Statistics
Type: Water
Height: 3'11" Weight: 55 lbs
Appearance: Unknown Dungeon and Route 23. Seafoam Islands (by fishing)
Description: Capable of swimming backwards by rapidly flapping its wing-like pectoral fins and stout tail.

Learned Skill List:

Level	Skill	Type
—	Bubble	Water
LV 19	Smokescreen	Normal
LV 24	Leer	Normal
LV 30	Water Gun	Water
LV 41	Agility	Psychic
LV 52	Hydro Pump	Water

Technical Machines: 06, 09, 10, 11, 12, 13, 14, 15, 20, 31, 32, 34, 39, 40, 44, 50
Hidden Machines: 03

Goldeen—No. 118

Evolution: No. 119 Seaking (LV 33)

Vital Statistics
Type: Water
Height: 2'0" Weight: 33 lbs
Appearance: Routes 4, 12, 13, 17, 18, 19, 20, 21, 22, 24, and 25; Cerulean City; Fuchsia City; Seafoam Islands; Cinnabar Island (by fishing)
Description: The Goldeen's tail fin billows like an elegant ballroom dress, giving it the nickname of the Water Queen.

Learned Skill List:

Level	Skill	Type
—	Peck	Flying
—	Tail Whip	Normal
LV 19	Supersonic	Normal
LV 24	Horn Attack	Normal
LV 30	Fury Attack	Normal
LV 37	Waterfall	Water
LV 45	Horn Drill	Normal
LV 54	Agility	Psychic

Technical Machines: 06, 07, 09, 10, 11, 12, 13, 14, 20, 31, 32, 34, 39, 40, 44, 50
Hidden Machines: 03

Seaking—No. 119

Evolution: Final Form

Vital Statistics
Type: Water
Height: 4'3" Weight: 86 lbs
Appearance: Fuchsia City, Route 23, Unknown Dungeon (by fishing)
Description: In the autumn spawning season, they can be seen swimming powerfully up rivers and creeks.

Learned Skill List:

Level	Skill	Type
—	Peck	Flying
—	Tail Whip	Normal
—	Supersonic	Normal
LV 24	Horn Attack	Normal
LV 30	Fury Attack	Normal
LV 39	Waterfall	Water
LV 48	Horn Drill	Normal
LV 54	Agility	Psychic

Technical Machines: 06, 07, 09, 10, 11, 12, 13, 14, 15, 20, 31, 32, 34, 39, 40, 44, 50
Hidden Machines: 03

Staryu—No. 120

Evolution: No. 121 Starmie (Water Stone)

Vital Statistics
Type: Water
Height: 2'7" Weight: 76 lbs
Appearance: Routes 19, 20, and 21; Seafoam Islands; Cinnabar Island (by fishing)
Description: An enigmatic Pokémon that can effortlessly regenerate any appendage it loses in battle.

Learned Skill List:

Level	Skill	Type
—	Tackle	Normal
LV 17	Water Gun	Water
LV 22	Harden	Normal
LV 27	Recover	Normal
LV 32	Swift	Normal
LV 37	Minimize	Normal
LV 42	Light Screen	Psychic
LV 47	Hydro Pump	Water

Technical Machines: 06, 09, 10, 11, 12, 13, 14, 20, 24, 25, 29, 30, 31, 32, 33, 34, 39, 40, 44, 45, 46, 49, 50
Hidden Machines: 03, 05

Starmie—No. 121

Evolution: Final Form

Vital Statistics
Type: Water/Psychic
Height: 3'7" Weight: 176 lbs
Appearance: —
Description: Its central core glows with the seven colors of the rainbow. Some people value the core as a gem.

Learned Skill List:

Level	Skill	Type
—	Tackle	Normal
—	Water Gun	Water
—	Harden	Normal

Technical Machines: 06, 09, 10, 11, 12, 13, 14, 15, 20, 24, 25, 29, 30, 31, 32, 33, 34, 39, 40, 44, 45, 46, 49, 50
Hidden Machines: 03, 05

Mr. Mime—No. 122

Evolution: Final Form

Vital Statistics
Type: Psychic
Height: 4'3" Weight: 120 lbs
Appearance: Route 2
Description: If interrupted while miming, Mr. Mime will slap the enemy around with its broad hands.

Learned Skill List:

Level	Skill	Type
—	Confusion	Psychic
—	Barrier	Psychic
LV 23	Light Screen	Psychic
LV 31	Double Slap	Normal
LV 39	Meditate	Psychic
LV 47	Substitute	Normal

Technical Machines: 01, 05, 06, 08, 09, 10, 15, 17, 18, 19, 20, 22, 24, 25, 29, 30, 31, 32, 33, 34, 35, 40, 44, 45, 46, 50
Hidden Machines: 05

Scyther—No. 123

Evolution: Final Form

Vital Statistics
Type: Bug/Flying
Height: 4'11" Weight: 123 lbs
Appearance: Safari Zone, Coin Exchange (Celadon City)
Description: With ninja-like agility and speed, the Scyther can create the illusion that there are more than one.

Learned Skill List:

Level	Skill	Type
—	Quick Attack	Normal
LV 17	Leer	Normal
LV 20	Focus Energy	Normal
LV 24	Double Team	Normal
LV 29	Slash	Normal
LV 35	Swords Dance	Normal
LV 42	Agility	Psychic

Technical Machines: 03, 06, 09, 10, 15, 20, 31, 32, 34, 39, 40, 44, 50
Hidden Machines: 01

Jynx—No. 124

Evolution: Final Form

Vital Statistics
Type: Ice/Psychic
Height: 4'7" Weight: 90 lbs
Appearance: Cerulean City
Description: It seductively wiggles its hips as it walks. The Jynx can cause people to dance in unison with it.

Learned Skill List:

Level	Skill	Type
—	Pound	Normal
—	Lovely Kiss	Normal
LV 15	Sing	Normal
LV 23	Double Slap	Normal
LV 31	Ice Punch	Ice
LV 39	Meditate	Normal
LV 47	Blizzard	Ice

Technical Machines: 01, 05, 06, 08, 09, 10, 11, 12, 13, 14, 15, 17, 18, 19, 20, 29, 30, 31, 32, 33, 34, 35, 40, 44, 46, 50
Hidden Machines: N/A

Electabuzz—No. 125

Evolution: Final Form

Vital Statistics
Type: **Electric**
Height: **3'7"** Weight: **66 lbs**
Appearance: Power Plant
Description: **Normally found near power plants, they can wander away and cause major blackouts in cities.**

Learned Skill List:

Level	Skill	Type
—	Quick Attack	Normal
—	Leer	Normal
LV 34	Thunder Shock	Electric
LV 37	Screech	Normal
LV 42	Thunder Punch	Electric
LV 49	Light Screen	Psychic
LV 54	Thunder	Electric

Technical Machines: 01, 05, 06, 08, 09, 10, 15, 17, 18, 19, 20, 24, 25, 29, 30, 31, 32, 33, 34, 35, 39, 40, 44, 45, 46, 50
Hidden Machines: 04, 05

Magmar—No. 126

Evolution: Final Form

Vital Statistics
Type: **Flame**
Height: **4'3"** Weight: **98 lbs**
Appearance: Pokémon House (Cinnabar Island)
Description: **Its body always burns with an orange glow that enables it to hide perfectly among flames.**

Learned Skill List:

Level	Skill	Type
—	Ember	Flame
LV 36	Leer	Normal
LV 39	Confuse Ray	Ghost
LV 43	Fire Punch	Flame
LV 48	Smokescreen	Normal
LV 52	Smog	Poison
LV 55	Flamethrower	Flame

Technical Machines: 01, 05, 06, 08, 09, 10, 15, 17, 18, 19, 20, 29, 30, 31, 32, 34, 35, 38, 40, 44, 46, 50
Hidden Machines: 04

Pinsir—No. 127

Evolution: Final Form

Vital Statistics
Type: **Bug**
Height: **4'11"** Weight: **121 lbs**
Appearance: Safari Zone, Coin Exchange (Celadon City)
Description: **If it fails to crush the victim in its pincers, the Pinsir will swing it around and toss it hard.**

Learned Skill List:

Level	Skill	Type
—	Vice Grip	Normal
LV 25	Seismic Toss	Fighting
LV 30	Guillotine	Normal
LV 36	Focus Energy	Normal
LV 43	Harden	Normal
LV 49	Slash	Normal
LV 54	Swords Dance	Normal

Technical Machines: 03, 06, 08, 09, 10, 15, 17, 19, 20, 31, 32, 34, 44, 50
Hidden Machines: 01

Tauros—No. 128

Evolution: Final Form

Vital Statistics
Type: **Normal**
Height: **4'7"** Weight: **195 lbs**
Appearance: Safari Zone
Description: **When the Tauros targets an enemy, it charges furiously while whipping its foe with its long tails.**

Learned Skill List:

Level	Skill	Type
—	Tackle	Normal
LV 21	Stomp	Normal
LV 28	Tail Whip	Normal
LV 35	Leer	Normal
LV 44	Rage	Normal
LV 51	Take Down	Normal

Technical Machines: 06, 07, 08, 09, 10, 13, 14, 15, 20, 24, 25, 26, 27, 31, 32, 34, 38, 40, 44, 50
Hidden Machines: 04

Magikarp—No. 129

Evolution: No, 130 Gyarados (LV 20)

Vital Statistics
Type: **Water**
Height: **2'11"** Weight: **22 lbs**
Appearance: Routes 12, 13, 17, and 18; Fuchsia City (by fishing)
Description: **In the distant past, the Magikarp was somewhat stronger than the weaker descendants that exist today.**

Learned Skill List:

Level	Skill	Type
—	Splash	Normal
LV 15	Tackle	Normal

Technical Machines: N/A
Hidden Machines: N/A

Gyarados—No. 130

Evolution: Final Form

Vital Statistics
Type: **Water/Flying**
Height: **21'4"** Weight: **518 lbs**
Appearance: —
Description: **Rarely seen in the wild. Huge and vicious, the Gyarados is capable of destroying entire cities in a rage.**

Learned Skill List:

Level	Skill	Type
LV 20	Bite	Normal
LV 25	Dragon Rage	Dragon
LV 32	Leer	Normal
LV 41	Hydro Pump	Water
LV 52	Hyper Beam	Normal

Technical Machines: 06, 08, 09, 10, 11, 12, 13, 14, 15, 20, 23, 24, 25, 31, 32, 33, 34, 38, 40, 44, 50
Hidden Machines: 03, 04

Lapras—No. 131

Evolution: Final Form

Vital Statistics
Type: **Water/Ice**
Height: **8'2"** Weight: **485 lbs**
Appearance: Saffron City
Description: **A Pokémon that has been over-hunted almost to extinction. It can ferry people over water.**

Learned Skill List:

Level	Skill	Type
—	Water Gun	Water
—	Growl	Normal
LV 16	Sing	Normal
LV 20	Mist	Ice
LV 25	Body Slam	Normal
LV 31	Confuse Ray	Ghost
LV 38	Ice Beam	Ice
LV 46	Hydro Pump	Water

Technical Machines: 06, 07, 08, 09, 10, 11, 12, 13, 14, 15, 20, 22, 23, 24, 25, 29, 31, 32, 33, 34, 40, 44, 46, 50
Hidden Machines: 03, 04

Ditto—No. 132

Evolution: Final Form

Vital Statistics
Type: **Normal**
Height: **1'0"** Weight: **9 lbs**
Appearance: Routes 13, 14, 15, and 23; Unknown Dungeon
Description: **Capable of copying an enemy's genetic code to transform itself instantly into a duplicate of the enemy.**

Learned Skill List:

Level	Skill	Type
—	Transform	Normal

Technical Machines: N/A
Hidden Machines: N/A

Eevee—No. 133

Evolution: Vaporeon (Water Stone); Jolteon (Thunder Stone); Flareon (Fire Stone)

Vital Statistics
Type: **Normal**
Height: **1'0"** Weight: **14 lbs**
Appearance: Celadon Mansion (Celadon City)
Description: **Its genetic code is irregular. It may mutate if it is exposed to radiation from elemental stones.**

Learned Skill List:

Level	Skill	Type
—	Tackle	Normal
—	Sand Attack	Normal
LV 27	Quick Attack	Normal
LV 31	Tail Whip	Normal
LV 37	Bite	Normal
LV 45	Take Down	Normal

Technical Machines: 06, 08, 09, 10, 20, 31, 32, 33, 34, 39, 40, 44, 50
Hidden Machines: N/A

Vaporeon—No. 134

Evolution: Final Form

Vital Statistics
Type: Water
Height: 3'3" Weight: 64 lbs
Appearance: —
Description: Lives close to water. Its long tail is ridged with a fin that is often mistaken for a mermaid's.

Learned Skill List:

Level	Skill	Type
—	Tackle	Normal
—	Sand Attack	Normal
LV 27	Quick Attack	Normal
LV 31	Water Gun	Water
LV 37	Tail Whip	Normal
LV 40	Bite	Normal
LV 42	Acid Armor	Poison
LV 44	Haze	Ice
LV 48	Mist	Ice
LV 54	Hydro Pump	Water

Technical Machines: 06, 08, 09, 10, 11, 12, 13, 14, 15, 20, 31, 32, 33, 34, 39, 40, 44, 50
Hidden Machines: 03

Jolteon—No. 135

Evolution: Final Form

Vital Statistics
Type: Electric
Height: 2'7" Weight: 54 lbs
Appearance: —
Description: The Jolteon accumulates negative ions in the atmosphere to blast out 10,000-volt lightning bolts.

Learned Skill List:

Level	Skill	Type
—	Tackle	Normal
—	Sand Attack	Normal
LV 27	Quick Attack	Normal
LV 31	Thunder Shock	Electric
LV 37	Tail Whip	Normal
LV 40	Thunderwave	Electric
LV 42	Double Kick	Fighting
LV 44	Agility	Psychic
LV 48	Pin Missile	Bug
LV 54	Thunder	Electric

Technical Machines: 06, 08, 09, 10, 15, 20, 24, 25, 31, 32, 33, 34, 39, 40, 44, 45, 50
Hidden Machines: 05

Flareon—No. 136

Evolution: Final Form

Vital Statistics
Type: Flame
Height: 2'11" Weight: 55 lbs
Appearance: —
Description: When storing thermal energy in its body, the Flareon's temperature can soar to over 1,600 degrees.

Learned Skill List:

Level	Skill	Type
—	Tackle	Normal
—	Sand Attack	Normal
LV 27	Quick Attack	Normal
LV 31	Ember	Flame
LV 37	Tail Whip	Normal
LV 37	Bite	Normal
LV 42	Leer	Normal
LV 44	Fire Spin	Flame
LV 48	Rage	Normal
LV 54	Flamethrower	Flame

Technical Machines: 06, 08, 09, 10, 15, 20, 31, 32, 33, 34, 38, 39, 40, 44, 50
Hidden Machines: N/A

Porygon—No. 137

Evolution: Final Form

Vital Statistics
Type: Normal
Height: 2'7" Weight: 80 lbs
Appearance: Coin Exchange (Celadon City)
Description: A Pokémon that consists entirely of programming code. Capable of moving freely in cyberspace.

Learned Skill List:

Level	Skill	Type
—	Tackle	Normal
—	Sharpen	Normal
—	Conversion	Normal
LV 23	Psybeam	Psychic
LV 28	Recover	Normal
LV 35	Agility	Psychic
LV 42	Tri-Attack	Normal

Technical Machines: 06, 09, 10, 13, 14, 15, 20, 24, 25, 29, 30, 31, 32, 33, 34, 39, 40, 44, 45, 46, 49, 50
Hidden Machines: 05

Omanyte—No. 138

Evolution: No. 139 Omastar (LV 40)

Vital Statistics
Type: Rock/Water
Height: 1'4" Weight: 17 lbs
Appearance: Helix Fossil
Description: Although long extinct, in rare cases the Omanyte can be genetically resurrected from fossils.

Learned Skill List:

Level	Skill	Type
—	Water Gun	Water
—	Withdraw	Water
LV 34	Horn Attack	Normal
LV 39	Leer	Normal
LV 46	Spike Cannon	Normal
LV 53	Hydro Pump	Water

Technical Machines: 06, 08, 09, 10, 11, 12, 13, 14, 20, 31, 32, 33, 34, 44, 50
Hidden Machines: 03

Omastar—No. 139

Evolution: Final Form

Vital Statistics
Type: Rock/Water
Height: 3'3" Weight: 77 lbs
Appearance: —
Description: A prehistoric Pokémon that died out when its heavy shell made it impossible to catch prey.

Learned Skill List:

Level	Skill	Type
—	Water Gun	Water
—	Withdraw	Water
—	Horn Attack	Normal
LV 39	Leer	Normal
LV 44	Spike Cannon	Normal
LV 49	Hydro Pump	Water

Technical Machines: 06, 07, 08, 09, 10, 11, 12, 13, 14, 15, 17, 19, 20, 31, 32, 33, 34, 40, 44, 50
Hidden Machines: 03

Kabuto—No. 140

Evolution: No. 141 Kabutops (LV 40)

Vital Statistics
Type: Rock/Water
Height: 1'8" Weight: 25 lbs
Appearance: Dome Fossil
Description: A Pokémon that was resurrected from a fossil found in what was once the ocean floor eons ago.

Learned Skill List:

Level	Skill	Type
—	Scratch	Normal
—	Harden	Normal
LV 34	Absorb	Grass
LV 39	Slash	Normal
LV 44	Leer	Normal
LV 49	Hydro Pump	Water

Technical Machines: 06, 08, 09, 10, 11, 12, 13, 14, 20, 31, 32, 33, 34, 44, 50
Hidden Machines: 03

Kabutops—No. 141

Evolution: Final Form

Vital Statistics
Type: Rock/Water
Height: 4'3" Weight: 89 lbs
Appearance: —
Description: The Kabutops' sleek shape is perfect for swimming. It slashes prey with its claws and drains the bodies.

Learned Skill List:

Level	Skill	Type
—	Scratch	Normal
—	Harden	Normal
—	Absorb	Grass
—	Slash	Normal
LV 46	Leer	Normal
LV 53	Hydro Pump	Water

Technical Machines: 02, 03, 05, 06, 08, 09, 10, 11, 12, 13, 14, 15, 17, 19, 20, 31, 32, 33, 34, 40, 44, 50
Hidden Machines: 03

Aerodactyl—No. 142

Evolution: Final Form

Vital Statistics
Type: Rock/Flying
Height: 5'11" Weight: 130 lbs
Appearance: Old Amber
Description: A ferocious prehistoric Pokémon that goes for the enemy's throat with its saw-like fangs.

Learned Skill List:

Level	Skill	Type
—	Wing Attack	Flying
—	Agility	Psychic
LV 33	Supersonic	Normal
LV 38	Bite	Normal
LV 45	Take Down	Normal
LV 54	Hyper Beam	Normal

Technical Machines: 02, 04, 06, 09, 10, 15, 20, 23, 31, 32, 33, 34, 38, 39, 43, 44, 50
Hidden Machines: 02

Snorlax—No. 143

Evolution: Final Form

Vital Statistics
Type: Normal
Height: 6'11" **Weight:** 1014 lbs
Appearance: Routes 12 and 16
Description: Very lazy, the Snorlax just eats and sleeps. As its rotund bulk builds, it becomes steadily more slothful.

Learned Skill List:

Level	Skill	Type
—	Headbutt	Normal
—	Amnesia	Psychic
—	Rest	Psychic
LV 35	Body Slam	Normal
LV 41	Harden	Normal
LV 48	Double Edge	Normal
LV 56	Hyper Beam	Normal

Technical Machines: 01, 05, 06, 08, 09, 10, 11, 12, 13, 14, 15, 16, 17, 18, 19, 20, 22, 24, 25, 26, 27, 29, 31, 32, 33, 34, 35, 36, 38, 40, 44, 46, 48, 50
Hidden Machines: 03, 04

Articuno—No. 144

Evolution: Final Form

Vital Statistics
Type: Ice/Flying
Height: 5'7" **Weight:** 122 lbs
Appearance: Seafoam Islands
Description: A legendary bird Pokémon that is said to appear to doomed people who are lost in icy mountains.

Learned Skill List:

Level	Skill	Type
—	Peck	Flying
—	Ice Beam	Ice
LV 51	Blizzard	Ice
LV 55	Agility	Psychic
LV 60	Mist	Ice

Technical Machines: 02, 04, 06, 09, 10, 11, 12, 13, 14, 15, 20, 31, 32, 33, 34, 39, 43, 44, 50
Hidden Machines: 02

Zapdos—No. 145

Evolution: Final Form

Vital Statistics
Type: Electric/Flying
Height: 5'3" **Weight:** 116 lbs
Appearance: Power Plant
Description: A legendary bird Pokémon that is said to appear from clouds while dropping enormous lightning bolts.

Learned Skill List:

Level	Skill	Type
—	Thunder Shock	Electric
—	Drill Peck	Flying
LV 51	Thunder	Electric
LV 55	Agility	Psychic
LV 60	Light Screen	Psychic

Technical Machines: 02, 04, 06, 09, 10, 15, 20, 24, 25, 31, 32, 33, 34, 39, 43, 44, 45, 50
Hidden Machines: 02, 05

Moltres—No. 146

Evolution: Final Form

Vital Statistics
Type: Flame/Flying
Height: 6'7" **Weight:** 132 lbs
Appearance: Victory Road
Description: Known as the legendary bird of fire. Every flap of its wings creates a dazzling flash of flames.

Learned Skill List:

Level	Skill	Type
—	Peck	Flying
—	Fire Spin	Flame
LV 51	Leer	Normal
LV 55	Agility	Psychic
LV 60	Sky Attack	Flying

Technical Machines: 02, 04, 06, 09, 10, 15, 20, 31, 32, 33, 34, 38, 39, 43, 44, 50
Hidden Machines: 02

Dratini—No. 147

Evolution: No. 148 Dragonair (LV 30), No. 149 Dragonite (LV 55)

Vital Statistics
Type: Dragon
Height: 5'11" **Weight:** 7 lbs
Appearance: Safari Zone (by fishing), Coin Exchange (Celadon City)
Description: Long considered a mythical Pokémon until recently when a small colony was found living underwater.

Learned Skill List:

Level	Skill	Type
—	Wrap	Normal
—	Leer	Normal
LV 10	Thunderwave	Electric
LV 20	Agility	Psychic
LV 30	Slam	Normal
LV 40	Dragon Rage	Dragon
LV 50	Hyper Beam	Normal

Technical Machines: 06, 08, 09, 10, 11, 12, 13, 14, 20, 23, 24, 25, 31, 32, 33, 34, 38, 39, 40, 44, 45, 50
Hidden Machines: 03

Dragonair—No. 148

Evolution: No. 149 Dragonite (LV 55)

Vital Statistics
Type: Dragon
Height: 13'1" **Weight:** 36 lbs
Appearance: —
Description: A mystical Pokémon that exudes a gentle aura. Has the ability to change climate conditions.

Learned Skill List:

Level	Skill	Type
—	Wrap	Normal
—	Leer	Normal
—	Thunderwave	Electric
LV 20	Agility	Psychic
LV 35	Slam	Normal
LV 45	Dragon Rage	Dragon
LV 55	Hyper Beam	Normal

Technical Machines: 06, 07, 08, 09, 10, 11, 12, 13, 14, 20, 23, 24, 25, 31, 32, 33, 34, 38, 39, 40, 44, 45, 50
Hidden Machines: 03

Dragonite—No. 149

Evolution: Final Form

Vital Statistics
Type: Dragon/Flying
Height: 7'3" **Weight:** 463 lbs
Appearance: —
Description: An rarely seen marine Pokémon. Its intelligence is said to match that of humans.

Learned Skill List:

Level	Skill	Type
—	Wrap	Normal
—	Leer	Normal
—	Thunderwave	Electric
—	Agility	Psychic
LV 35	Slam	Normal
LV 45	Dragon Rage	Dragon
LV 60	Hyper Beam	Normal

Technical Machines: 02, 06, 07, 08, 09, 10, 11, 12, 13, 14, 15, 20, 23, 24, 25, 31, 32, 33, 34, 38, 39, 40, 44, 45, 50
Hidden Machines: 03, 04

Mewtwo—No. 150

Evolution: Final Form

Vital Statistics
Type: Psychic
Height: 6'7" **Weight:** 269 lbs
Appearance: Unknown Dungeon
Description: It was created by a scientist after years of horrific gene splicing and DNA engineering.

Learned Skill List:

Level	Skill	Type
—	Confusion	Psychic
—	Disable	Normal
—	Swift	Normal
LV 63	Barrier	Psychic
LV 66	Psychic	Psychic
LV 70	Recover	Normal
LV 75	Mist	Ice
LV 81	Amnesia	Psychic

Technical Machines: 01, 05, 06, 08, 09, 10, 11, 12, 13, 14, 15, 17, 18, 19, 20, 22, 24, 25, 29, 30, 31, 32, 33, 34, 35, 36, 38, 40, 44, 45, 46, 49, 50
Hidden Machines: 04, 05

Appendix A

All the Skills You Ever Need to Know

Raising Pokémon can be confusing work—especially when you find yourself having to pick and choose between a bunch of skills. Each Pokémon retains the knowledge of up to four skills at once. To learn more than that, your Pokémon is going to have to forget something! Use this list of skills to help you determine which skills to keep and which to get rid of.

Name of Skill	TM #	Type	Pow	Acc	PP
Absorb		Grass	20	100	20
Acid		Poison	40	100	30
Acid Armor		Poison		100	40
Agility		Psychic		100	30
Amnesia		Psychic		100	20
Aurora Beam		Ice	65	100	20
Barrage		Normal	15	85	20
Barrier		Psychic		100	30
Bide	34	Normal		100	10
Bind		Normal	15	75	20
Bite		Normal	60	100	25
Blizzard	14	Ice	120	90	5
Body Slam	8	Normal	85	100	15
Bone Club		Ground	65	85	20
Bonemerang		Ground	50	90	10
Bubble		Water	20	100	30
Bubblebeam	11	Water	65	100	20
Clamp		Water	35	75	10
Comet Punch		Normal	18	85	15
Confuse Ray		Ghost		100	10
Confusion		None	50	100	25
Constrict		Normal	10	100	35
Conversion		Normal		100	30
Counter	18	Fighting		100	20
Crabhammer		Water	90	85	10
Cut	HM01	Normal	50	95	30
Defense Curl		Normal		100	40
Dig	28	Ground	60	100	10
Disable		Normal		55	20
Dizzy Punch		Normal	70	100	10
Double-Edge	10	Normal	100	100	15
Double Kick		Fighting	30	100	30
Double Slap		Normal	15	85	10
Double Team	32	Normal		100	15
Dragon Rage	23	Dragon		100	10
Dream Eater	42	Psychic	100	100	15
Drill Peck		Flying	80	100	20
Earthquake	26	Ground	100	100	10
Egg Bomb	37	Normal	100	75	10
Ember		Fire	40	100	25
Explosion	47	Normal	250	100	5
Fire Blast	38	Fire	120	85	5
Fire Punch		Fire	75	100	15
Fire Spin		Fire	15	70	15
Fissure	27	Ground		30	5
Flamethrower		Fire	95	100	15
Flash	HM05	Normal		70	20
Fly	HM02	Flying	70	95	15
Focus Energy		Normal		100	30
Fury Attack		Normal	15	85	20
Fury Swipes		Normal	18	80	15
Glare		Normal		75	30
Growl		Normal		100	40
Growth		Normal		100	40
Guillotine		Normal		30	5
Gust		Flying	40	100	35
Harden		Normal		100	30
Haze		Ice		100	30
Headbutt		Normal	70	100	15
High Jump Kick		Fighting	85	90	20
Horn Attack		Normal	65	100	25
Horn Drill	7	Normal		30	5
Hydro Pump		Water	120	80	5
Hyper Beam	15	Normal	150	90	5
Hyper Fang		Normal	80	90	15
Hypnosis		Psychic		60	20
Ice Beam	13	Ice	95	100	10
Ice Punch		Ice	75	100	15
Jump Kick		Fighting	70	95	25
Karate Chop		Normal	50	100	25
Kinesis		Psychic		80	15

Description

The player absorbs HP from the enemy equal to half of the attack damage.
Normal attack with a 10 % chance of lowering your opponent's defense.
Doubles your Pokémon's defense strength.
Doubles your Pokémon's speed.
Doubles your Pokémon's special abilities.
Normal attack with a 10 % chance of lowering your opponent's attack strength. May also freeze your opponent.
Player's Pokémon attacks two to five times in a row.
Doubles your Pokémon's defense strength.
Player's Pokémon loses two to three turns, then attacks the enemy with twice the total damage they received.
Player's Pokémon attacks two to five times in a row, during which the enemy can't counterattack.
Normal attack with a 10 % chance of scaring the enemy, making him unable to attack.
Normal attack with a 30 % chance of freezing your enemy.
Normal attack with a 30 % chance of paralyzing your enemy.
Normal attack with a 10 % chance of scaring the enemy, making him unable to attack.
Player's Pokémon attacks twice in a row.
Normal attack with a 10 % chance of lowering the enemy's speed.
Normal attack with a 10 % chance of lowering the enemy's speed.
Player's Pokémon attacks two to five times in a row, during which the enemy can't counterattack.
Player's Pokémon attacks two to five times in a row.
Confuses the enemy.
Normal attack with a 10 % chance of confusing the enemy.
Normal attack with a 10 % chance of lowering the enemy's speed.
Your Pokémon's element becomes the same as the enemy's.
The player's Pokémon inflicts double the damage they received on their next turn. This works only against physical attacks!
If successful, it causes a critical hit.
Normal attack.
Raises your Pokémon's defense.
First, your Pokémon digs into the ground, then on the second turn, it attacks.
Seals up one of your enemy's special skills.
Normal attack.
The player takes damage equal to one-quarter of what the opponent receives.
Player's Pokémon attacks twice in a row.
Player's Pokémon attacks two to five times in a row.
It increases your Pokémon's chances of evading attacks.
Takes exactly 40 points of damage from the enemy.
While the enemy sleeps, the player absorbs its hit points.
Normal attack.
Normal attack that has no effect on flying Pokémon.
Normal attack.
Normal attack with a 10 % chance of burning the enemy.
Destroys the enemy in one hit.
Normal attack with a 20 % chance of burning the enemy.
Normal attack with a 10 % chance of burning the enemy.
Player's Pokémon attacks two to five times in a row, during which the enemy can't counterattack.
When successful, the enemy is automatically defeated. Doesn't work on flying
Normal attack with a 10 % chance of burning the enemy.
Lowers the enemy's accuracy.
The Pokémon flies into the air and then attacks on Turn Two.
If successful, causes a critical hit.
Player's Pokémon attacks two to five times in a row.
Player's Pokémon attacks two to five times in a row.
Paralyzes enemy, if successful.
Decreases the enemy's attack strength.
Increases your Pokémon's special abilities.
If successful, the enemy is automatically defeated.
Normal Attack
Increases your Pokémon's defense.
Makes the enemy unable to determine whether you are friend or foe. Removes all attack support effects.
Normal attack with a 30 % chance of scaring the enemy, making him or her unable to attack.
If the player's Pokémon misses, it takes one-eighth of the damage that was to be dealt to the enemy.
Normal attack.
If successful, the enemy is automatically defeated.
Normal attack.
Pokémon inflicts a great amount of damage but loses the next turn.
Normal attack with a 10 % chance of scaring the enemy, making him unable to attack.
Puts enemy to sleep.
Normal attack with a 10 % chance of freezing the enemy.
Normal attack with a 10 % chance of freezing the enemy.
If the player's Pokémon misses, it takes one-eighth of the damage that was to be dealt to the enemy.
Causes a critical hit.
Decreases the enemy's accuracy.

Name of Skill	TM #	Type	Pow	Acc	PP
Leech Life		Bug	20	100	15
Leech Seed		Grass		90	10
Leer		Normal		100	30
Lick		Ghost	20	100	30
Light Screen		Psychic		100	30
Lovely Kiss		Normal		75	10
Low Kick		Fighting	50	90	20
Meditate		Psychic		100	40
Mega Drain	21	Grass	40	100	10
Mega Kick	5	Normal	120	75	5
Mega Punch	1	Normal	80	85	20
Metronome	35	Normal		100	10
Mimic	31	Normal		100	10
Minimize		Normal		100	20
Mirror Move		Flying		100	20
Mist		Ice		100	30
Night Shade		Ghost		100	15
Pay Day	16	Normal	40	100	20
Peck		Flying	35	100	35
Petal Dance		Grass	70	100	20
Pin Missile		Bug	14	85	20
Poison Gas		Poison		55	40
Poison Sting		Poison	15	100	35
Poisonpowder		Poison		75	35
Pound		Normal	40	100	35
Psybeam		Psychic	65	100	20
Psychic	29	Psychic	90	100	10
Psywave	46	Psychic		80	15
Quick Attack		Normal	40	100	30
Rage	20	Normal	20	100	20
Razor Leaf		Grass	55	95	25
Razor Wind	2	Normal	80	75	10
Recover		Normal		100	20
Reflect	33	Psychic		100	20
Rest	44	Psychic		100	10
Roar		Normal		100	20
Rock Slide	48	Rock	75	90	10
Rock Throw		Rock	50	65	15
Rolling Kick		Fighting	60	85	15
Sand Attack		Normal		100	15
Scratch		Normal	40	100	30
Screech		Normal		85	40
Seismic Toss	19	Fighting		100	20
Self Destruct	36	Normal	200	100	5
Sharpen		Normal		100	30
Sing		Normal		55	15
Skull Bash	40	Normal	100	100	15
Sky Attack	43	Flying	140	90	5
Slam		Normal	80	75	20
Slash		Normal	70	100	20
Sleep Powder		Grass		75	15
Sludge		Poison	65	100	20
Smog		Poison	20	70	20
Smokescreen		Normal		100	20
Softboiled	41	Normal	50	100	10
Solarbeam	22	Grass	120	100	20
Sonic Boom		Normal		90	20
Spike Cannon		Normal	20	100	15
Splash		Normal		100	40
Spore		Grass		100	15
Stomp		Normal	65	100	20
Strength	HM04	Normal	80	100	15
String Shot		Bug		95	40
Struggle		Normal	50	100	
Stun Spore		Grass		75	30
Submission	17	Fighting	80	80	25
Substitute	50	Normal		100	10
Super Fang		Normal		90	10

Description

Absorbs the enemy's hit points.

Every turn, the player's Pokémon absorbs the enemy's hit points.

Lowers the enemy's defenses.

Normal attack with a 30 % chance of paralyzing the enemy.

Halves the damage you receive from special attacks.

Puts enemy to sleep.

Normal attack with a 30 % chance of scaring the enemy, making him unable to attack.

Increases your Pokémon's attack strength.

The player absorbs HP from the enemy equal to half of the attack damage.

Normal attack.

Normal attack.

Produces various attacks randomly.

Your Pokémon can use the opponent's attacks.

Shrinks Pokémon, increasing its ability to evade attacks.

Pokémon performs the same attack as the enemy's Pokémon.

Pokémon is defended against any enemy attacks that try to lower its abilities.

The enemy takes damage equal to the Pokémon's level.

After the fight ends, the player receives Pokémon currency.

Normal attack.

After the second or third attack, the player's Pokémon becomes confused.

Player's Pokémon attacks two to five times in a row.

If successful, the enemy is poisoned.

Normal attack with a 20 % chance of poisoning the enemy.

If successful, the enemy is poisoned.

Normal attack.

Normal attack with a 10 % chance of confusing the enemy.

Normal attack with a 10 % chance of reducing the enemy's special skills.

Damage dealt to enemy is equal to one to one and a half times your Pokémon's experience level.

The player's Pokémon attacks first without fail.

As the Pokémon takes damage, its attack points increase. They continue to increase until the battle ends.

If successful, it causes a critical hit.

Pokémon stores power during the first turn, then attacks during the second.

Player's Pokémon recovers half of its maximum hit points.

Reduces the damage the player's Pokémon receives by half. Works only on physical attacks.

Recover 100 %% of HP but lose two turns afterwards.

Automatically ends the battle. Only works on wild Pokémon.

Normal attack.

Normal attack.

Normal attack with a 30 % chance of scaring the enemy, making him unable to attack.

Lowers enemy's accuracy.

Normal attack.

Greatly lowers enemy's defenses.

The amount of damage inflicted upon the enemy is equal to the level of the player's Pokémon.

Highly damaging attack that makes the Pokémon who uses it faint, taking it out of the battle.

Increases the Pokémon's attack strength.

Puts the enemy to sleep.

Pokémon ducks his head during Turn One and attacks for Turn Two.

Gathers strength for a turn and attacks during the next.

Normal attack.

Causes a critical hit.

Puts enemy to sleep.

Normal attack with a 40 % chance of poisoning the enemy.

Attack that poisons the enemy, if successful.

Lowers enemy's accuracy.

Recover one-half of maximum hit points.

Stores solar power for the first turn then attacks on the second.

Always does 20 points of damage to the enemy.

Pokémon attacks two to five times in a row.

Pokémon jumps.

Puts enemy to sleep.

Normal attack with a 30 % chance of scaring the enemy, making him unable to attack.

Normal attack.

Lowers enemy's speed.

If all PP is gone, this technique can be used. However, the Pokémon using Struggle will receive one-quarter of the damage dealt out.

If successful, enemy may be paralyzed.

The player takes damage equal to one-quarter of what the opponent receives.

Pokémon clones itself. With each clone, it takes one-quarter of the original Pokémon's HP and applies it to the clone. The clones then fight automatically.

Reduces enemy's hit points by half.

Name of Skill	TM #	Type	Pow	Acc	PP
Supersonic		Normal		55	20
Surf	HM03	Water	95	100	15
Swift	39	Normal	60	100	20
Swords Dance	3	Normal		100	30
Tackle		Normal	35	95	35
Tail Whip		Normal		100	30
Take Down	9	Normal	90	85	20
Teleport	30	Psychic			20
Thrash		Normal	90	100	20
Thunder	25	Electric	120	70	10
Thunder Wave	45	Electric		100	20
Thunderbolt	24	Electric	95	100	15
Thunder Punch		Electric	75	100	15
Thundershock		Electric	40	100	30
Toxic	6	Poison		85	10
Transform		Normal		100	10
Tri Attack	49	Normal	80	100	10
Twineedle		Bug	25	100	20
Vice Grip		Normal	55	100	30
Vine Whip		Grass	35	100	10
Water Gun	12	Water	40	100	25
Waterfall		Water	80	100	15
Whirlwind	4	Normal		85	20
Wing Attack		Flying	60	100	35
Withdraw		Water		100	40
Wrap		Normal	5	85	20

Appendix B

Items Galore!

As you travel through the world of *Pokémon*, you'll encounter numerous items, many of which are crucial to completing your quest. If you find yourself stuck because you can't find something, or wondering what certain items can do, take a look at the tables below.

Remedies and Other Medicines

Item Name	Cost	Location	Function
POTION	300P	Poké Marts	Heals up to 20 HP.
SUPER POTION	700P	Poké Marts	Heals up to 50 HP.
HYPER POTION	1,200P	Poké Marts	Heals up to 200HP.
MAX POTION	2,500P	Poké Marts	Complete HP recovery!
FULL RESTORE	3,000P	Poké Marts	Recovers all HP and cures any status problems.
REVIVE	1,500P	Poké Marts	Resurrects fainted Pokémon and heals half of their HP.
MAX REVIVE	—	Item Balls in dungeons and routes	Resurrection and complete HP recovery.
ANTIDOTE	100P	Poké Marts	Cures poisoned Pokémon.
AWAKENING	250P	Poké Marts	Wakens sleeping Pokémon.
BURN HEAL	250P	Poké Marts	Heals burned Pokémon.
ICE HEAL	250P	Poké Marts	Thaws frozen Pokémon.
PARALYZ HEAL	200P	Poké Marts	Frees paralyzed Pokémon.
FULL HEAL	600P	Poké Marts	Cures your Pokémon of any status problem, other than "Faint."

Description

Confuses the enemy, if successful.
Normal attack.
Attack hits 100 % of the time.
Increases Pokémon's attack strength.
Normal attack.
Decreases enemy's defense.
The player takes damage equal to one-quarter of what the opponent receives.
Teleports Pokémon out of battle, ending it. Doesn't work against trainers' Pokémon.
On its second or third turn, the player's Pokémon becomes confused.
Normal attack with 10 % chance of paralyzing the enemy.
Paralyzes enemy.
Normal attack that paralyzes enemy.
Normal attack with 10% chance of paralyzing enemy.
Normal attack with 10% chance of paralyzing enemy.
Every turn, the poison's damage increases.
Player's Pokémon turns into opponent's Pokémon.
Normal attack.
The player's Pokémon attacks twice in a row with a chance at poisoning enemy.
Normal attack.
Normal attack.
Normal attack.
Normal attack.
Automatically ends battle. Doesn't work against other trainers.
Normal attack.
Increases Pokémon's defense.
Player's Pokémon attacks two to five times in a row.

Vitamins and Other Power-Ups

Item Name	Cost	Location	Function
HP UP	—	Item Balls in dungeons and routes	Raises the maximum number of HP
CALCIUM	9,800P	Celadon Dept. Store (Fifth Floor)	Raises the Pokémon's special power.
CARBOS	9,800P	Celadon Dept. Store (Fifth Floor)	Raises the Pokémon's speed.
IRON	9,800P	Celadon Dept. Store (Fifth Floor)	Raises the Pokémon's defense strength.
PROTEIN	9,800P	Celadon Dept. Store (Fifth Floor)	Raises the Pokémon's attack strength.
RARE CANDY	—	Item Balls in dungeons and routes	Raises the Pokémon up one level.

For Use In Battle Only

Item Name	Cost	Location	Function
DIRE HIT	950P	Celadon Dept. Store (Fifth Floor)	Increases the Pokémon's critical hit percentage.
GUARD SPEC.	700P	Celadon Dept. Store (Fifth Floor)	Protects the Pokémon from the enemies' special attacks.
X ACCURACY	650P	Celadon Dept. Store (Fifth Floor)	Raises the Pokémon's accuracy.
X ATTACK	500P	Celadon Dept. Store (Fifth Floor)	Raises the Pokémon's attack strength.
X DEFEND	550P	Celadon Dept. Store (Fifth Floor)	Raises the Pokémon's defense strength.
X SPEED	350P	Celadon Dept. Store (Fifth Floor)	Raises the Pokémon's speed.
X SPECIAL	350P	Celadon Dept. Store (Fifth Floor)	Raises the Pokémon's special power.

PP Potions

Item Name	Cost	Location	Function
ELIXIR	—	Item Balls in dungeons and routes	Restores 10PP on all of the Pokémon's skills.
ETHER	—	Item Balls in dungeons and routes	Restores 10PP on one of the Pokémon's skills.
MAX ELIXIR	—	Item Balls in dungeons and routes	Restores all PP on all of the Pokémon's skills.
MAX ETHER	—	Item Balls in dungeons and routes	Restores all PP on one of the Pokémon's skills.
PP UP	—	Item Balls in dungeons and routes	Raises the maximum number of PP.

Beverages

Item Name	Cost	Location	Function
FRESH WATER	200P	Celadon Dept. Store (Rooftop)	Heals up to 50HP.
SODA POP	300P	Celadon Dept. Store (Rooftop)	Heals up to 60HP.
LEMONADE	350P	Celadon Dept. Store (Rooftop)	Heals up to 80HP.

Necessary Tools

Item Name	Cost	Location	Function
POKé BALL	200P	Poké Marts	Basic tool for catching wild Pokémon.
GREAT BALL	600P	Poké Marts	More effective at capturing Pokémon than the Poké Ball.
ULTRA BALL	1,200P	Poké Marts	Has the highest capture ratio of all the Monster Balls that you can purchase in a Poké Mart.
SAFARI BALL	—	Safari Zone	Monster Balls used exclusively in the Safari Zone.
MASTER BALL	—	Saffron City (Silph Co.)	The ultimate Monster Ball! This captures 100 percent of the time, *but* you only get one of them.
BICYCLE	1,000,000P	Cerulean City (Bike Shop)	An expensive bike that you can use to travel around faster or in areas like Cycling Road.
ESCAPE ROPE	550P	Poké Marts	A magical rope which pulls you out of a cave or gym and takes you to the last Pokémon Center visited.
POKé DOLL	1,000P	Celadon Dept. Store (Fourth Floor)	A popular Pokémon doll that distracts enemy Pokémon and makes them want to flee!
REPEL	350P	Poké Marts	A spray repellent that keeps wild Pokémon at bay for a short amount of time (about 100 steps). Your lead Pokémon's level determines whether your other Pokémon will be attacked. Any Pokémon with a level which is lower than the lead Pokémon's will be attacked.
SUPER REPEL	500P	Poké Marts	A more powerful spray that protects you from random attacks for about 200 steps.
MAX REPEL	700P	Poké Marts	The most powerful repellent on the market. Protects you for 250 steps.

Mysterious Stones and Fossils

Item Name	Cost	Location	Function
DOME FOSSIL	—	Mt. Moon	Give it to a scientist on Cinnabar Island and he'll turn it into a Kabuto.
HELIX FOSSIL	—	Mt. Moon	Give it to a scientist on Cinnabar Island and he'll turn it into an Omanyte.
OLD AMBER	—	Pewter City (Museum Annex)	Give it to a scientist on Cinnabar Island and he'll turn it into an Aerodactyl.
FIRE STONE	2,100P	Celadon Dept. Store (Fourth Floor)	Used to evolve certain Fire Pokémon.
LEAF STONE	2,100P	Celadon Dept. Store (Fourth Floor)	Used to evolve certain Plant Pokémon.
MOON STONE	—	Mt. Moon, Route 2, Celadon City (Game Corner Basement)	Used to evolve certain Magical Pokémon like the Clefairy or Jigglypuff.
THUNDER STONE	2,100P	Celadon Dept. Store (Fourth Floor)	Used to evolve certain Electric Pokémon.
WATER STONE	2,100P	Celadon Dept. Store (Fourth Floor)	Used to evolve certain Water Pokémon.

Miscellaneous—but Important—Items

Item Name	Cost	Location	Function
BOULDER BADGE	—	Pewter City Gym	Increases the attack strength of all your Pokémon and allows you to use Flash outside of battle.
CASCADE BADGE	—	Cerulean City Gym	Makes Pokémon up to level 30 obey you and allows you to use Cut outside of battle.
EARTH BADGE	—	Viridian City Gym	All Pokémon will obey you!
MARSH BADGE	—	Saffron City Gym	Makes Pokémon up to level 70 obey you.
RAINBOW BADGE	—	Celadon City Gym	Makes Pokémon up to level 50 obey you and allows you to use Strength outside of battle.
SOUL BADGE	—	Fuchsia City Gym	Increases the defense strength of all of your Pokémon and lets you use Surf outside of battle.
THUNDER BADGE	—	Vermilion City Gym	Increases the speed of all of your Pokémon and lets you use Fly outside of battle.
VOLCANO BADGE	—	Cinnabar Island Gym	Increases the special power of all of your Pokémon.
BIKE VOUCHER	—	Vermilion City	Coupon good for one free bike.
CARD KEY	—	Saffron City (Silph Co)	Special card used to open locked doors in the Silph Co. Building.
COIN CASE	—	Celadon City	Holds special coins used for playing the slot machines in the Game Corner.
EXP. ALL	—	Route 15 (Gate House to Fuchsia City)	Distributes EXP points to all of the Pokémon in your party, even if they don't fight in a battle.
GOLD TEETH	—	Safari Zone	Give to Safari Zone Director in exchange for HM04 (Strength).

Item Name	Cost	Location	Function
ITEMFINDER	—	Route 11 (Gate House to Route 12)	A tool which detects hidden items on the screen.
LIFT KEY	—	Celadon City (Team Rocket Hideout)	Activates the elevator in Team Rocket's Hideout.
NUGGET	—	Item Balls in dungeons and routes	Sell at a Poké Mart for 5,000P.
OAK'S PARCEL	—	Viridian City	Deliver to Prof. Oak in exchange for a Pokédex.
POKé FLUTE	—	Pokémon Tower	Wakes sleeping Pokémon.
POKéDEX	—	Prof. Oak's Lab.	Used to track information about the Pokémon you've captured or seen.
OLD ROD	—	Vermilion City	Used to catch a single kind of Water Pokémon, the Magikarp.
GOOD ROD	—	Fuchsia City	Can use to catch up to two types of Water Pokémon.
SUPER ROD	—	Route 12	The best fishing pole available! Use to catch any kind of Water Pokémon available.
S.S. TICKET	—	Route 25	Given to you by Bill to attend the party on the *S.S. Anne*.
SECRET KEY	—	Pokémon House	Needed to enter the locked Gym on Cinnabar Island.
SILPH SCOPE	—	Celadon City (Team Rocket Hideout)	Allows you to see the true form of the ghosts in Pokémon Tower.
TOWN MAP	—	Pallet Town	A map given to you by your rival's sister which allows you to view all of the Pokémon world.

Technical and Hidden Machines

Item Name	Cost	Location	Skill Learned
TM #01	3,000P	Celadon Dept. Store (Second Floor), Mt. Moon	Mega Punch
TM #02	2,000P	Celadon Dept. Store (Second Floor), Celadon City (Team Rocket Hideout)	Razor Wind
TM #03	—	Saffron City (Silph Co.)	Swords Dance
TM #04	—	Route 4	Whirlwind
TM #05	3,000P	Celadon Dept. Store (Second Floor), Victory Road	Mega Kick
TM #06	—	Fuchsia City Gym	Toxic
TM #07	2,000P	Celadon Dept. Store (Second Floor), Celadon City (Team Rocket Hideout)	Horn Drill
TM #08	—	*S.S. Anne*	Body Slam
TM #09	3,000P	Celadon Dept. Store (Second Floor), Saffron City (Silph Co.)	Take Down
TM #10	—	Celadon City (Team Rocket Hideout)	Double-Edge
TM #11	—	Cerulean City Gym	Bubblebeam
TM #12	—	Mt. Moon	Water Gun
TM #13	—	Celadon Dept. Store (Rooftop)	Ice Beam
TM #14	—	Pokémon House	Blizzard
TM #15	—	Celadon Coin Exchange (5500 coins)	Hyper Beam
TM #16	—	Route 12	Pay Day
TM #17	3,000P	Celadon Dept. Store (Second Floor), Victory Road	Submission
TM #18	—	Celadon Dept. Store (Third Floor Counter)	Counter
TM #19	—	Route 25	Seismic Toss
TM #20	—	Route 15 (Gate House to Fuchsia City)	Rage
TM #21	—	Celadon City Gym	Mega Drain
TM #22	—	Pokémon House	Solarbeam
TM #23	—	Celadon Coin Exchange (3300 coins)	Dragon Rage
TM #24	—	Vermilion City Gym	Thunderbolt
TM #25	—	Power Plant	Thunder
TM #26	—	Saffron City (Silph Co.)	Earthquake
TM #27	—	Viridian City Gym	Fissure
TM #28	—	Cerulean City	Dig
TM #29	—	Saffron City	Psychic
TM #30	—	Route 9	Teleport
TM #31	—	Saffron City	Mimic
TM #32	1000P	Celadon Dept. Store (Second Floor), Safari Zone	Double Team
TM #33	1,000P	Celadon Dept. Store (Second Floor), Power Plant	Reflect
TM #34	—	Pewter City Gym	Bide
TM #35	—	Cinnabar Island	Metronome
TM #36	—	Saffron City (Silph Co.)	Self Destruct

Item Name	Cost	Location	Skill Learned
TM #37	2,000P	Celadon Dept. Store (Second Floor), Safari Zone	Egg Bomb
TM #38	—	Cinnabar Island Gym	Fire Blast
TM #39	—	Route 12 (Gate House)	Swift
TM #40	—	Safari Zone	Skull Bash
TM #41	—	Celadon City	Softboiled
TM #42	—	Viridian City	Dream Eater
TM #43	—	Victory Road	Sky Attack
TM #44	—	S.S. Anne	Rest
TM #45	—	Route 24	Thunder Wave
TM #46	—	Saffron City Gym	Psywave
TM #47	—	Victory Road	Explosion
TM #48	—	Celadon Dept. Story (Rooftop)	Rock Slide
TM #49	—	Celadon Dept. Story (Rooftop)	Tri Attack
TM #50	—	Celadon Coin Exchange (7000 coins)	Substitute
HM #01	—	S.S. Anne	Cut
HM #02	—	Route 16	Fly
HM #03	—	Safari Zone	Surf
HM #04	—	Fuchsia City	Strength
HM #05	—	Route 2	Flash

Appendix c

A Pokémon Check-List

To keep you focused, we've included this handy checklist so that you can keep track of which Pokémon you've captured.

Caught It!	No.	Name
☐	001	BULBASAUR
☐	002	IVYSAUR
☐	003	VENUSAUR
☐	004	CHARMANDER
☐	005	CHARMELEON
☐	006	CHARIZARD
☐	007	SQUIRTLE
☐	008	WARTORTLE
☐	009	BLASTOISE
☐	010	CATERPIE
☐	011	METAPOD
☐	012	BUTTERFREE
☐	013	WEEDLE
☐	014	KAKUNA
☐	015	BEEDRILL
☐	016	PIDGEY
☐	017	PIDGEOTTO
☐	018	PIDGEOT
☐	019	RATTATA
☐	020	RATICATE
☐	021	SPEAROW
☐	022	FEAROW
☐	023	EKANS
☐	024	ARBOK
☐	025	PIKACHU
☐	026	RAICHU
☐	027	SANDSHREW
☐	028	SANDSLASH
☐	029	NIDORAN ♀
☐	030	NIDORINA
☐	031	NIDOQUEEN
☐	032	NIDORAN ♂
☐	033	NIDORINO
☐	034	NIDOKING
☐	035	CLEFAIRY
☐	036	CLEFABLE

Caught It!	No.	Name
☐	037	VULPIX
☐	038	NINETALES
☐	039	JIGGLYPUFF
☐	040	WIGGLYTUFF
☐	041	ZUBAT
☐	042	GOLBAT
☐	043	ODDISH
☐	044	GLOOM
☐	045	VILEPLUME
☐	046	PARAS
☐	047	PARASECT
☐	048	VENONAT
☐	049	VENOMOTH
☐	050	DIGLETT
☐	051	DUGTRIO
☐	052	MEOWTH
☐	053	PERSIAN
☐	054	PSYDUCK
☐	055	GOLDUCK
☐	056	MANKEY
☐	057	PRIMEAPE
☐	058	GROWLITHE
☐	059	ARCANINE
☐	060	POLIWAG
☐	061	POLIWHIRL
☐	062	POLIWRATH
☐	063	ABRA
☐	064	KADABRA
☐	065	ALAKAZAM
☐	066	MACHOP
☐	067	MACHOKE
☐	068	MACHAMP
☐	069	BELLSPROUT
☐	070	WEEPINBELL
☐	071	VICTREEBEL
☐	072	TENTACOOL
☐	073	TENTACRUEL
☐	074	GEODUDE
☐	075	GRAVELER
☐	076	GOLEM
☐	077	PONYTA
☐	078	RAPIDASH
☐	079	SLOWPOKE
☐	080	SLOWBRO

Caught It!	No.	Name
☐	081	MAGNEMITE
☐	082	MAGNETON
☐	083	FARFETCH'D
☐	084	DODUO
☐	085	DODRIO
☐	086	SEEL
☐	087	DEWGONG
☐	088	GRIMER
☐	089	MUK
☐	090	SHELLDER
☐	091	CLOYSTER
☐	092	GASTLY
☐	093	HAUNTER
☐	094	GENGAR
☐	095	ONIX
☐	096	DROWZEE
☐	097	HYPNO
☐	098	KRABBY
☐	099	KINGLER
☐	100	VOLTORB
☐	101	ELECTRODE
☐	102	EXEGGCUTE
☐	103	EXEGGUTOR
☐	104	CUBONE
☐	105	MAROWAK
☐	106	HITMONLEE
☐	107	HITMONCHAN
☐	108	LICKITUNG
☐	109	KOFFING
☐	110	WEEZING
☐	111	RHYHORN
☐	112	RHYDON
☐	113	CHANSEY
☐	114	TANGELA
☐	115	KANGASKHAN
☐	116	HORSEA
☐	117	SEADRA
☐	118	GOLDEEN
☐	119	SEAKING
☐	120	STARYU
☐	121	STARMIE
☐	122	MR.MIME
☐	123	SCYTHER

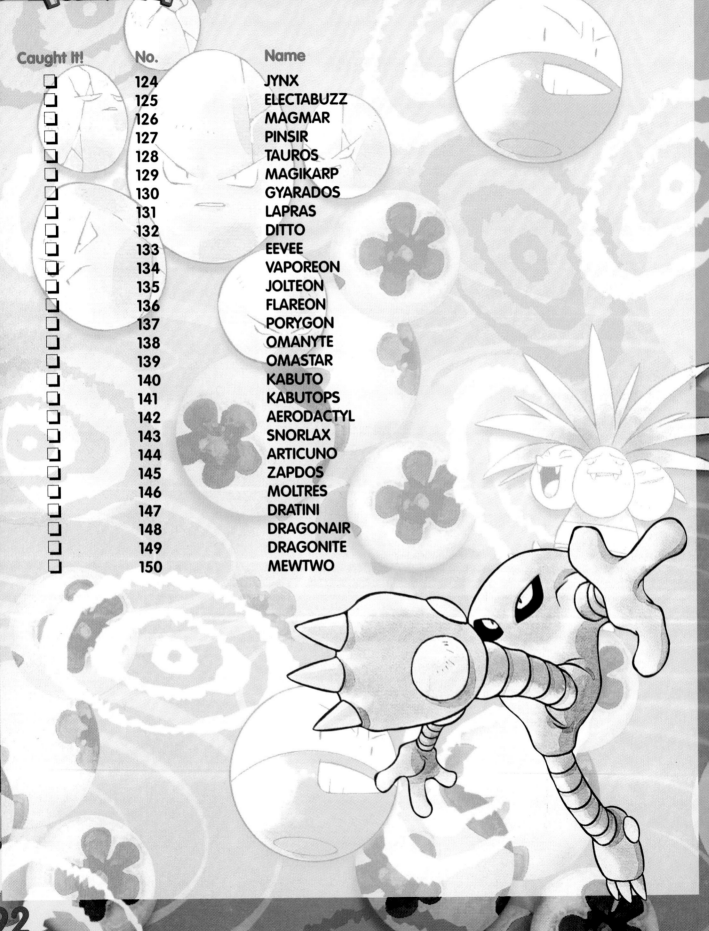

Caught It!	No.	Name
☐	124	JYNX
☐	125	ELECTABUZZ
☐	126	MAGMAR
☐	127	PINSIR
☐	128	TAUROS
☐	129	MAGIKARP
☐	130	GYARADOS
☐	131	LAPRAS
☐	132	DITTO
☐	133	EEVEE
☐	134	VAPOREON
☐	135	JOLTEON
☐	136	FLAREON
☐	137	PORYGON
☐	138	OMANYTE
☐	139	OMASTAR
☐	140	KABUTO
☐	141	KABUTOPS
☐	142	AERODACTYL
☐	143	SNORLAX
☐	144	ARTICUNO
☐	145	ZAPDOS
☐	146	MOLTRES
☐	147	DRATINI
☐	148	DRAGONAIR
☐	149	DRAGONITE
☐	150	MEWTWO

(GOT YA!)